First Published—July 1974

ISBN 0 85524 168 3 (Hard Cover Edition)

ISBN 0 85524 169 1 (Paper Cover Edition)

Printed in Great Britain by
Chapel River Press, Andover, Hants SP10 3NS,
for the Publishers, Almark Publishing Co. Ltd.,
49 Malden Way, New Malden,
Surrey KT3 6EA, England.

Introduction

IT has been my intention, within the confines of this book, to record as fully as possible the uniforms worn by the Royal Armoured Corps. The book deals specifically with the period 1970–1972 and so covers what must be the final amalgamation within the Corps, ie, The Royal Scots Greys and the 3rd Carabiniers into the Royal Scots Dragoon Guards. It was this occasion that prompted me to compile this reference. Most of the uniforms described have been in use for some years previous to 1970 and in fact Full Dress in the majority of cases dates from 1900, and no doubt will be worn for several years to come. But some of the traditional uniforms are gradually disappearing, eg, No 1 Dress (Blues) and in all probability will not be renewed when they have worn out. As it is, 'Blues' are no longer regulation and are retained by the regiments for certain personnel only. It is an historical fact that regimental tradition is stronger than a War Office order and it is this that makes the study of military uniform so frustrating and, at the same time, one of the most interesting aspects of military history.

The material in this book has been compiled from Army Regulations, Regimental Dress Standing Orders, Regimental Journals and invaluable help of individuals serving in the Royal Armoured Corps.

CONTENTS **Page**

The Life Guards

FULL DRESS: SCARLET.
FACING COLOUR: BLUE.
PLUME: WHITE.
NO. 1 DRESS: BLUE.
FACING COLOUR: BLUE.

Although it is not, strictly speaking, part of the Royal Armoured Corps, no book on the cavalry regiments would be complete without mentioning the Household Division. In this brief book I have tried to describe all the orders of dress of these complex regiments. Inevitably though, some information is bound to be left out. Where possible, throughout the book, all uniform details have been taken from the individual regiments' dress regulations.

Officers

MOUNTED REVIEW ORDER. Steel helmet with gilt fittings and white horsehair plume. The garter of the Guard Star is enamelled blue and the cross is red. Brass chin scales which the Life Guards wear under the bottom lip. Scarlet tunic with dark blue collar and cuffs embroidered with gilt wire, blue piping and brass buttons. Steel cuirass with brass studs around the edge and brass shoulder scales. A gold waist belt holds the two halves of the cuirass together. Gold shoulder cords with aiguilettes around the right arm. White leather breeches, black jackboots, steel spurs and chains. The cartouche belt is gold lace with a centre red stripe.

THE STATE SWORD. This sword, made by Wilkinson, was first supplied to the officers of the 1st Life Guards in 1834 and adopted by the Horse Guards in 1874. It has been used by the officers of the Household Division ever since. The grip is black shark skin bound with silver wire and the guard is of steel with the Regimental Cypher and Crown embossed in brass. The blade is 39½ inches long and engraved with battle honours. The inside of the guard and the sword knot are white leather.

HORSE FURNITURE. State saddlery, collar chain, shabraque, review order breast plate, gold bridoon rein, goatskin, cloak and holsters.

DISMOUNTED REVIEW ORDER. See 'Dress regulations'.
Dark blue overalls with two red stripes with a red piping in between.

GUARD ORDER (SUMMER). See 'The Blues and Royals'.

GUARD ORDER (WINTER). See 'The Blues and Royals'.
The cloak is scarlet with a blue collar and gold gorget patches.

LEVEE DRESS. See 'Dress regulations'.

UNDRESS 'A'. See 'Dress regulations'.

UNDRESS 'B'. See 'Dress regulations'.

HORSE FURNITURE. Regimental headkit with brass headstall and

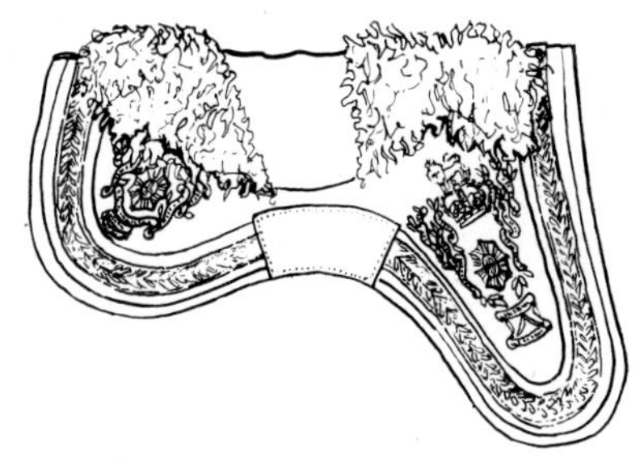

Officers' Shabraque: Dark blue with a wide scarlet band and a narrower gold lace band down the middle of it, dark blue edge. Gold embroidery with silver guard stars, white goat skin.

Life Guards button and regimental cypher.

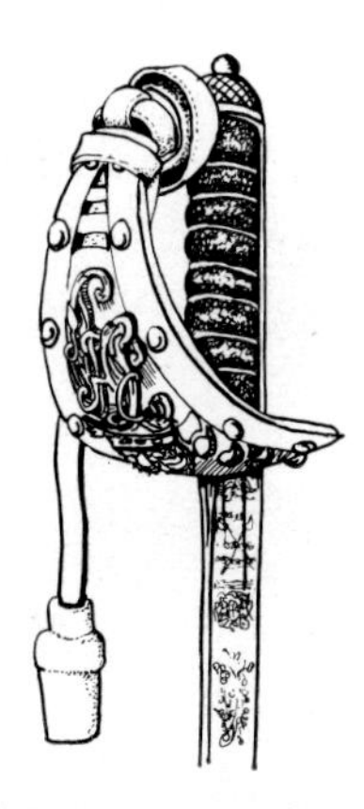

The state sword of officers of the Household Cavalry.

Major in Undress 'A'. Frock coat is all black. Note lace on arm.

stripped saddle, collar chain and Guard Order breastplate. Life Guard bearskin.

NO. 1 DRESS (CEREMONIAL). See 'Dress regulations'.

SERVICE DRESS. As the Blues and Royals except that the inside leg of the breeches is primrose and the breeches themselves are sand coloured twill. Brown boots and a red lanyard around the right shoulder.

HORSE FURNITURE. Regimental saddlery with universal bits and white headrope.

KHAKI DRILL (ABROAD). As the Blues and Royals.

SHIRT SLEEVE ORDER. As the Blues and Royals. The stable belt is red/blue/red and buckles are worn on the left side.

Remount rider (spur badge) exercising a new horse. RIGHT: Rear view of tunics: Farrier on the right and RCM on the left. Note the different pouch to the RQMC in the centre of the photo.

Soldiers

MOUNTED REVIEW ORDER. Helmet with white plume. Scarlet tunic with dark blue collar and cuffs trimmed with gold braid, blue piping and brass buttons. White breeches, black jackboots with steel swansneck spurs. Steel cuirass with brass fittings and white waistbelt. The rest of the uniform is as the Blues and Royals, as is the horse furniture except that the sheepskin is white and has a black scalloped edge.

DISMOUNTED REVIEW ORDER. See 'Dress regulations'.
The overalls have double scarlet stripes with scarlet piping between.

QUEEN'S LIFE GUARD (WINTER). See 'Dress regulations'.

FRONT YARD ORDER. See 'Dress regulations',

WALKING OUT ORDER. See 'Dress regulations'.

NO. 1 DRESS (CEREMONIAL). See 'Dress regulations'.

NO. 1 DRESS. See 'Dress regulations'.

NO. 1 DRESS (MOUNTED). See 'Dress regulations'.

NO. 2 DRESS. Forage cap. No. 2 dress khaki tunic and trousers. Brass buttons and shoulder titles reading—Life Guards. White waistbelt with brass plate bearing Royal Coat of Arms. Black boots or shoes.

NO. 2 DRESS (MOUNTED). See 'Dress regulations'.

KHAKI DRILL (ABROAD). As the Blues and Royals except that the Life Guard stable belts and hose tops are red/blue/red.

SHIRT SLEEVE ORDER. See 'Dress regulations'.

COMBAT DRESS, ETC. Standard issue. A black nylon polo-necked sweater can be worn under overalls in the tank park or on exercise.

FARRIERS. Black horsehair plume on the helmet. Dark blue tunic and a special crossbelt which houses the axe when it is not held in the hand. The belt has the traditional red flask cord worn by all the Household Cavalry. Farriers never wear cuirasses.

BANDSMEN. Musicians have special lace on their collars and cuffs and plaited gold cord epaulettes. (See colour plate.) They also have gold piping on the tunic, in place of the normal dark blue. Trumpeters have red plumes and, like the farriers, do not wear cuirasses. Musicians are mounted on brown horses and trumpeters on greys.

The Blues and Royals

FULL DRESS: BLUE.
FACING COLOUR: SCARLET.
PLUME: RED.
NO. 1 DRESS: BLUE.
FACING COLOUR: BLUE.
AMALGAMATION: 29TH MARCH 1969—THE ROYAL HORSE GUARDS AND THE 1ST ROYAL DRAGOONS.

Officers

MOUNTED REVIEW ORDER. Steel dragoon helmet with gilt badge and fittings and red horse hair plume. The centre of the guard star is enamelled with a blue garter and a red cross, this being the same as that of the Life

Detail close-up of Blues and Royals bridlery.

Trumpeters and a Corporal of Horse in dismounted review order. Note that there are two banners on the trumpets, the same design on both sides. The trumpeter on the left is also a Corporal of Horse.

(*N. Stafford*).

Guards. The Blues and Royals wear the chin chain under the chin and the Life Guards under the bottom lip. Dark blue tunic, red collar and cuffs embroidered with gold wire, and red piping down the front, around the bottom and up the back of the skirt. Brass buttons. Steel cuirass with brass studs around the edge and brass shoulder scales. A gold waist belt holds the two halves of the cuirass together. Gold woven shoulder cords and aiguillettes,

1. Brass (staybrite) shoulder strap badge—No. 2 Dress.

2. Gold wire arm badge—worn on the left upper arm on Full Dress.

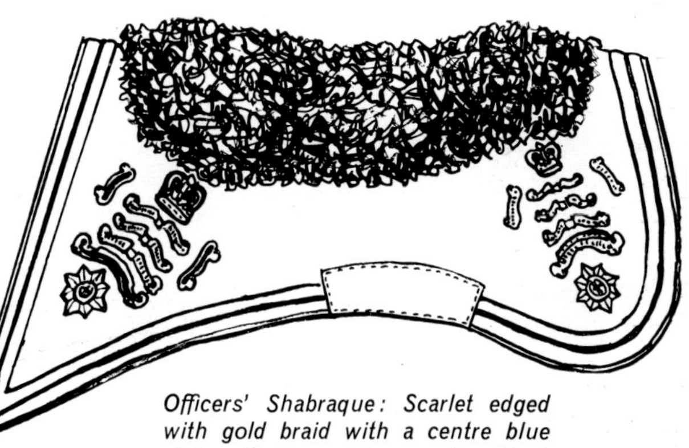

Officers' Shabraque: Scarlet edged with gold braid with a centre blue stripe. Gold on blue scrolls. Black skin.

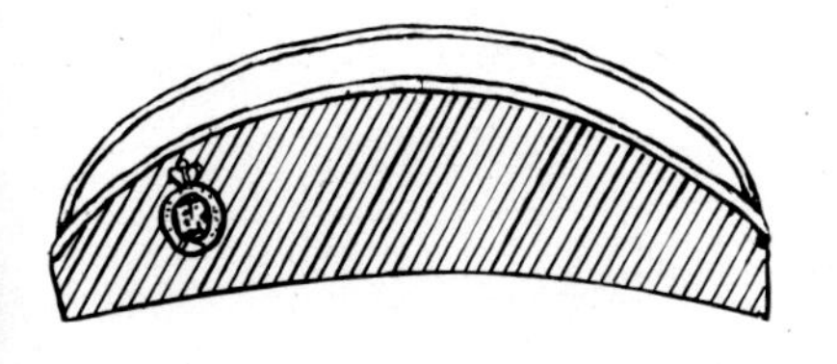

Side hat which can be worn when not on duty. The lower part and crown are dark blue. The rest is scarlet with yellow piping.

Regimental policeman. The armband is dark blue with the Household Cavalry badge between the red letters. The cuffs of the gauntlets, which are standard throughout the Army, are grey and white stripes.

which for officers are worn on the right. White leather breeches, black jackboots and steel spurs and chains. The cartouche belt is of gold lace with a centre stripe and edging of crimson. The buckle, slide, chape andt he cartouche itself are of engraved gilt metal. The State Sword and scabbard are of steel, with a white leather lining to the hilt and a white leather sword knot terminating in an acorn. The sword is suspended from gold sword slings. The belt is worn under the tunic. The uniform is completed with white gauntlet gloves.

HORSE FURNITURE. State saddlery, collar chain shabraque, beard, Guard Order breast plate, black bridoon rein, lambskin, cloak and holsters.

DISMOUNTED REVIEW ORDER. See 'Dress regulations'.
The overalls are dark blue with a wide red stripe down the sides.

GUARD ORDER (SUMMER). Helmet and plume, tunic with white cartouche belt and aiguillettes. Cuirass, leather breeches, jackboots and spurs. Gauntlet gloves. State Sword with white slings. For the '4 o'clock' inspection of the guard the cuirass is not worn.

HORSE FURNITURE. State saddlery, collar chain, sheepskin, Guard. Order breast plate, black bridoon rein, cloak and holsters.

GUARD ORDER (WINTER). As above, except that the cloak is worn instead of the cuirass and short white gloves are substituted for the gauntlets. The cloak is dark blue fastened with six brass buttons. It has a scarlet collar with large gold gorget patches, and a half belt at the back with two brass buttons which holds the back of the cloak in pleats when on foot, but which is taken off when mounted.

HORSE FURNITURE. As for Guard Order (Summer) but minus the cloaks.

LEVEE DRESS. See 'Dress regulations'.

UNDRESS 'A'. See 'Dress regulations'.

UNDRESS 'B'. See 'Dress regulations'.

HORSE FURNITURE. As for the Life Guards but with the addition of a sheepskin.

NO. 1 DRESS (CEREMONIAL). See 'Dress regulations'.

SERVICE DRESS. Forage or SD cap, SD jacket with a dark blue lanyard around the left shoulder, 'Sam Browne' belt, breeches of a slate grey khaki cavalry twill colour with the inside of the leg slate grey. Black field boots, spurs, whip or stick. The Blues and Royals carry a whip with a thong. Trousers with turn-ups are worn when not on mounted duty. Officers in service dress in the United Kingdom wear forage caps except on training. WO II and above have a dark blue backing to the cap badge, ie inside the garter and behind the Royal Cypher.

HORSE FURNITURE. Brown leather headkit and blue web girths, white headropes. No brass headstalls, wallets, breast plates or stirrup bosses.

KHAKI DRILL (ABROAD). Forage cap or service dress cap, bush shirt, cloth belt, trousers or shorts, brown shoes, stick or whip. Metal badges of rank, and lanyards. Khaki stockings are worn with shorts and the trousers can be Bedford cord or drill.

SHIRT SLEEVE-ORDER. Khaki open-necked shirt. Metal badges of rank. 'Sam Browne' belt or stable belt (blue/red/blue) with buckles to the front. Stick or whip.

Soldiers

MOUNTED REVIEW ORDER. Helmet and red plume, dark blue tunic with red collar and cuffs trimmed with gold braid, red piping, brass buttons and the gold Waterloo Eagle on the left upper arm. White breeches, black jackboots with steel swans-neck spurs. Steel cuirass with brass fittings and white waistbelt. White cartouche belt with crimson flask cord down the centre, brass fittings and a black pouch with a brass Royal Coat of Arms badge backed with red. Gold aiguillettes for Warrant Officers and Non-Commissioned Officers worn round the left arm. Sword with white slings and white gauntlet gloves. In wet weather a dark blue cloak with a red collar is worn.

HORSE FURNITURE. Household cavalry saddlery, collar chain, breast plate, black sheepskin, rolled cloak in the front arch of the saddle.

DISMOUNTED REVIEW ORDER. See 'Dress regulations'.
The overalls have a broad red stripe down the sides.

QUEEN'S LIFE GUARD (WINTER). See 'Dress regulations'.
The blue cloak with a red collar. The horse furniture is as mounted review order, less the cloak.

FRONT YARD ORDER. See 'Dress regulations'.

WALKING OUT DRESS. See 'Dress regulations'.

NO. 1 DRESS (CEREMONIAL). See 'Dress regulations'.

NO. 1 DRESS. See 'Dress regulations'.

NO. 1 DRESS (MOUNTED). See 'Dress regulations'.

NO. 2 DRESS. Forage cap. No. 2 dress tunic with brass buttons and shoulder titles reading—'BLUES and ROYALS'. A brass eagle is worn above the shoulder title on the flaps. White waist belt with a brass buckle plate bearing the Royal Coat of Arms. A white lanyard around the left shoulder. Black boots or shoes.

NO. 2 DRESS (MOUNTED). See 'Dress regulations'.

SHIRT SLEEVE ORDER. See 'Dress regulations'.

KHAKI DRILL (ABROAD). Forage cap or SD cap, which for soldiers is all khaki, including the peak. (It is also worn by recruits under riding tuition.) A lightweight cotton khaki dress shirt, similar in design to the khaki flannel type. White waist belt or stable belt (blue/red/blue), shorts or trousers and boots. When shorts are worn there is a special regimental sock which is khaki with a blue/red/blue horizontal stripe, turnover top.

COMBAT DRESS, ETC. Standard except that the beret badge is bronze, and black nylon polo necked sweaters can be worn under coveralls. In fact the Household Division are the only regiments that wear this.

FARRIERS. Unlike the Life Guards, Farriers of the Blues and Royals wear a red plume on their helmets. The cuffs of the tunic are dark blue edged with gold braid with a red inset to the gold chevron. (See photo in 'Dress regulations'). A gold horseshoe badge on a red patch is worn on the right upper arm.

BANDSMEN. All musicians of the Blues and Royals wear red plumes. The tunic is piped in gold and has special lace on the collar and cuffs.

Trumpeters have no buttons on the pocket flaps at the back of the tunic, but they retain the two just below the waist belt. They also have a special cloak, which is crimson with two broad stripes of gold lace down the front edges and a wide band of gold round the dark blue collar. Trumpeters are mounted on grey horses.

Dress Regulations—Household Cavalry

Officers

MOUNTED REVIEW ORDER. State occasions, escorts to the Sovereign and members of the Royal Family, lining the staircase of the Royal Palaces and the House of Lords, state funerals.

Helmet and plume, tunic, gold belt and aiguillettes, cuirasses, leather breeches, jackboots and spurs, gauntlet gloves. State sword with gold slings.

HORSE FURNITURE. See 'Life Guards' and 'Blues and Royals'.

DISMOUNTED REVIEW ORDER. (STATE OCCASIONS).

Helmet and plume, tunic, gold waist belt and aiguillettes, overalls, wellington boots (which are similar to a Chelsea boot and are worn under, and not over, the trousers) and spurs, gauntlet gloves. State sword and gold slings. The white cartouche belt and white sword slings are worn when members of the Royal Family are *not* present.

GUARD ORDER (SUMMER). The Queen's Life Guard and funerals of Field Marshals. Same as mounted review order, except that all belts and slings are white.

GUARD ORDER (WINTER). Same as above but with the addition of the cloak, and with short white gloves in place of the gauntlet gloves.

LEVEE DRESS. Levees and all state occasions when so ordered. Gold Stick and Silver Stick in-Waiting, and Silver Stick Adjutant when in attendance at Courts, Court Balls and the State Opening of Parliament.

Helmet and plume, tunic, gold belt and aiguilettes. Leather breeches, jackboots and spurs. Gauntlet gloves, state sword with gold slings.

UNDRESS 'A'. Garden parties at Windsor Castle. Silver Stick in-Waiting if received by the Sovereign other than on state occasions. Forage cap, frock coat, white waist belt, overalls, wellington boots and spurs. Short white gloves. State sword with white slings.

RIGHT: Blues and Royals helmets. LEFT: Life Guards helmet (Officers' and WOs pattern with the enamelled garter and cross). Note that the plume on the Life Guards' helmet is crimped in at the top.

Household Cavalry horse furniture. All leather work dark brown leather, browband and girth white. Badges, buckles and the decoration on the band behind the ears are brass. Stirrups, bit, rings and chain are steel. The Blues and Royals do not have a scalloped edge to the fur.

UNDRESS 'B'. Competing at horse shows and as ordered.

Forage cap, patrol jacket, white cartouche belt, pantaloons (riding breeches), butcher or hessian boots, spurs, short gloves, stick or whip.

UNDRESS 'C'. The orderly officer's inspection of the short guard at Whitehall. As for undress 'A'.

NO. 1 DRESS (CEREMONIAL). On dismounted ceremonial parades.

Forage cap, patrol jacket with gold shoulder cords. White belt, overalls, wellington boots and spurs. Short white gloves. Sword and white slings.

The badges of rank in this order of dress are in silver. For an investiture no State sword is worn and the straps are linked together.

NO. 1 DRESS. Forage cap, patrol jacket, white cartouche belt, overalls, wellington boots and spurs. Short white gloves. Badges of rank in this order are in gold on blue shoulder straps.

SERVICE DRESS. Forage or service cap, service dress jacket, 'Sam Browne' belt, breeches with slate grey strappings for the Blues and Royals and primrose for the Life Guards. (Trousers with turn-ups may be worn when dismounted). Spurs, whip or stick.

OTHER ORDERS OF DRESS, ie drill, shirt sleeve, combat, etc, are similar to all other units, and will be amply explained in other parts of the book. The dress regulations of the Life Guards and the Blues and Royals are extremely complex. Thus what has been written above is more or less the regimental standing orders and is best explained by looking at the illustrations.

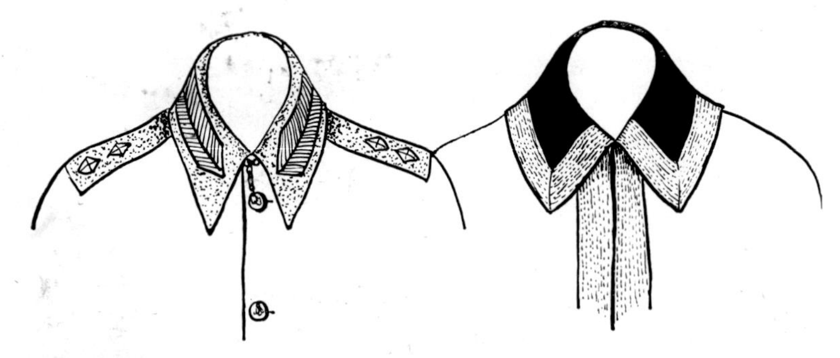

ABOVE RIGHT: Officers' cloak with gold gorget patches on the collar. Shoulder straps for the Blues and Royals are dark blue not red. LEFT: Trumpeters' cloak: crimson with dark blue collar and gold lace.

Soldiers

MOUNTED REVIEW ORDER. See officers' section for occasions when this order of dress is worn.

Helmet and plume, tunic, cuirass, white cartouche belt. Aiguillettes for warrant and non-commissioned ranks worn on the left. White breeches, jackboots and spurs, gauntlets, state sword with white sword knot and slings.

DISMOUNTED REVIEW ORDER. (See officers).

Helmet and plume, tunic, white cartouche belt, white waist belt, aiguillettes for WOs and NCOs, overalls, wellington boots, spurs, gauntlets and sword in white slings suspended from the belt.

QUEEN'S LIFE GUARD (WINTER). The cloak is worn over the tunic with short white gloves instead of gauntlets.

FRONT YARD ORDER—QUEEN'S LIFE GUARD (SUMMER). NCOs posting sentries in the front yard and the sentry on the entrance ot the Queen's quarters. The Queen's Life Guard turning out dismounted.

Helmet and plume, tunic, white cartouche belt, aiguillettes for WOs and NCOs, white waist belt, white breeches, jackboots and spurs, gauntlets, sword and white slings.

FRONT YARD ORDER—QUEEN'S LIFE GUARD (WINTER). As for Queen's Life Guard Order (winter) less cuirass and sword scabbard.

WALKING OUT ORDER. Forage cap, tunic, aiguillettes for WOs and NCOs, white waist belt, overalls, wellington boots and spurs, short white gloves, white slings linked.

NO. 1 DRESS (CEREMONIAL). Inspections and ceremonial parades.

Forage cap, patrol jacket, (this is another name for the No. 1 dress blue tunic, which differs slightly from the line cavalry type), gold edged shoulder straps, white cartouche belt, overalls, wellington boots and spurs, white gloves, state sword with white slings.

NO. 1 DRESS. Forage cap, patrol jacket, blue shoulder straps, white cartouche belt, overalls, wellington boots and spurs, white gloves.

NO. 1 DRESS (MOUNTED). Competing in horse shows.

Forage cap, patrol jacket, white cartouche belt, pantaloons, knee boots and spurs, white gloves.

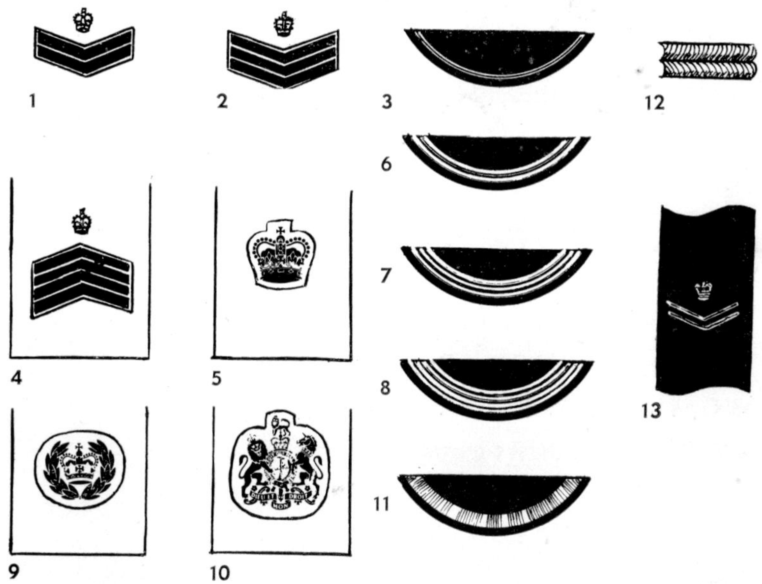

The rank distinctions of the Household Cavalry. 1. L/Cpl. or Full Cpl. After Sept 1971 L/Cpl. only. 2. Cpl. of Horse and after Sept. 1971 L/Cpl. of Horse. 3. Trooper. 4. Staff Cpl. or Squadron Quartermaster Cpl. 5. Squadron Cpl. major L. G. small crown. B C R Large crown. 6. L/Cpl. or Full Cpl. 7. Full Cpl. of Horse. 8. Staff Cpl. or S.Q.M.C. 9. Orderly room, regimental or technical Quartermaster Corporal. 10. Regimental Corporal Major. 11. R.C.M. and officers. 12 & 13. Detail of Braid used for Cap Peaks and No. 1 Dress rank chevrons.

NO. 2 DRESS. Non-ceremonial parades and routine duties.

Forage cap, No. 2 dress tunic and trousers, white waist belt, boots or shoes.

NO. 2 DRESS (MOUNTED). Forage cap, No. 2 dress tunic, pantaloons, knee boots and spurs. Worn in riding school or on sword instruction.

BUCKINGHAM PALACE ORDERLIES. By the Household Cavalry orderlies at Buckingham Palace or other royal residences.

Forage cap, patrol jacket, white cartouche belt, blue trousers, ankle boots, white gloves, blue mackintosh coat.

KHAKI DRILL. Abroad, as for No. 2 dress.

Forage or service dress cap, dress shirt, white waist belt or stable belt, shorts or trousers, boots. Life Guard or Blues and Royals hose tops worn with shorts.

SHIRT SLEEVE ORDER. Forage cap, khaki shirt, white waist belt or stable belt, No. 2 trousers, boots or shoes. Badges of rank are worn on arm or wrist band.

Denims are worn in stables, on musketry or maintenance parades.

Regimental buttons are worn on greatcoats, which are British warm greatcoats except in the case of WOIs who wear leather ones.

WOs and NCOs wear chevrons with brass crowns on their No. 2 tunics WOIIs of the Life Guards wear small brass crowns and WOIIs of the Blues and Royals wear larger ones.

An interesting custom retained by the Household Cavalry is their old rank names, a legacy from the days of Charles Stuart (later Charles II) when they were a body of gentlemen who went into exile with him and returned with him in 1660. At that time their NCOs ranked equal with officers of other corps. They are Corporal Major (Sergeant-Major), Quartermaster Corporal Major (Quartermaster Sergeant), Squadron Corporal Major (Squadron Sergeant Major), Corporal of Horse (Sergeant) and Corporal.

1st The Queen's Dragoon Guards

NO. 1 DRESS: BLUE.

FACING COLOUR: BLUE.

AMALGAMATION: 1ST JANUARY 1959—1ST THE KING'S DRAGOON GUARDS AND THE QUEEN'S BAYS (2ND DRAGOON GUARDS).

00CC75

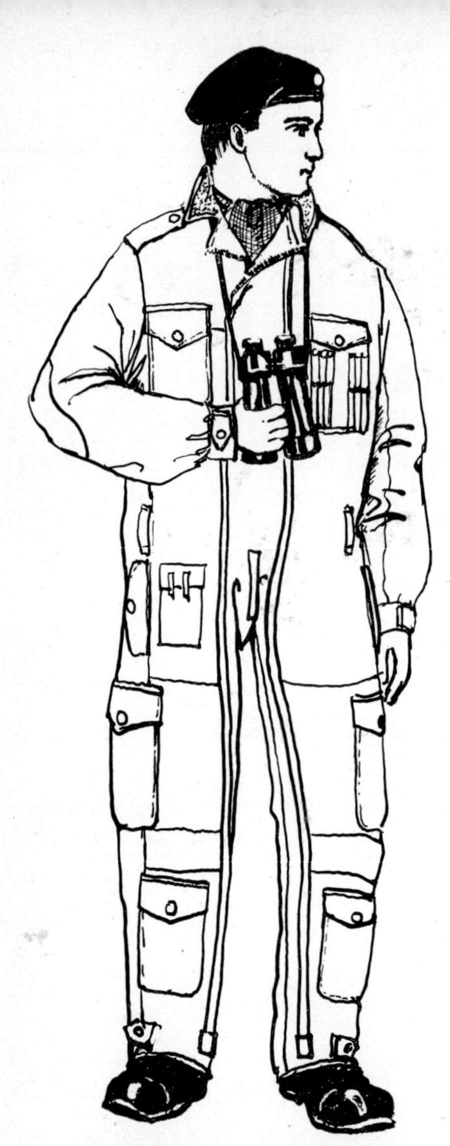

The tank suit illustrated was first introduced in 1943. It is made of heavy duty waterproof cotton lined with khaki angola wool shirt material. There are two full length zips down the front, strengthened shoulder straps for hauling the wearer out of the vehicle in emergencies, and numerous pockets. It is also strengthened at the knee, elbow and seat. A detachable hood can be press-studded to the collar. It is seen in various shades of light khaki and there is a camouflage version. Both the commander and driver of the Ferret scout car, shown on page 17, are wearing the 1943 pattern tank suit.

FULL DRESS. See plate, page 36. The pouch is black with a 'Bays' badge. The overalls are dark blue with a white stripe. The dragoon helmet is brass with a red plume for troopers and white for the band. The chin chains are worn under the bottom lip. Black boots and swan necked spurs. The sword, when carried, is the 1908 pattern with a white leather sword knot.

NO. 1 DRESS. All dark blue with a single white stripe down the sides of the trousers. Brass buttons down the front and on the breast pockets. Chain-mail on the shoulders with brass QDG badges. Brass 'Bays' collar badges, gold chevrons (right arm only) with a gold wire 'Bays' arm badge above for SQMSs, sergeants and corporals. The forage cap is dark blue with the cap band and piping in velvet and the badge in silver. Officers, when wearing No. 1 Dress during bad weather, can wear a short cloak. The tropical version (No. 3 Dress) is the same cut but the tunic is of white drill. Bandsmen wear a gold bandsman's lyre on the right arm above their rank chevrons, if any, or under

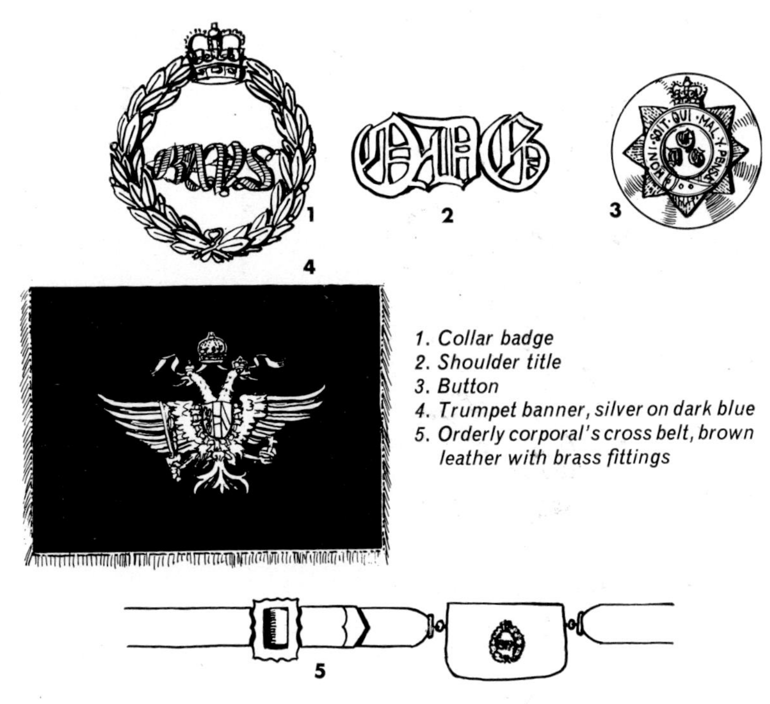

1. Collar badge
2. Shoulder title
3. Button
4. Trumpet banner, silver on dark blue
5. Orderly corporal's cross belt, brown leather with brass fittings

the warrant officer's badge. They also wear deep yellow woollen aiguilettes with brass finials around the left arm. They wear overalls and steel swan necked spurs. During inclement weather a short cloak of dark blue, lined with cobalt blue silk, is worn. It is fastened with three brass buttons.

NO. 2 DRESS. Standard issue with QDG shoulder titles, 'Bays' collar badges and a white lanyard around the right arm. Forage cap and black boots. The side hat, which is white with a dark blue body, flaps, peak and tip, may be worn for walking out dress. The Regimental arm badge, which is a brass 'Bays' surrounded by a wreath under which is a scroll, is worn on a cobalt blue backing. In the case of Staff Sergeants (SQMS) it is worn between the three chevrons and the crown. (This applies to all regiments.) In the case of the QDG the brass crowns on both arms are backed by cobalt blue felt. SQMSs also wear a khaki cord lanyard instead of the plaited white one. The waist belt is white leather with a silver beltplate and Eagle badge. The Regimental Provost (Police) arm band is dark blue with the letters RP in red, between which is the regiment's badge. When worn with No. 2 Dress it is at the very bottom of the left sleeve.

OFFICERS' SERVICE DRESS. The tunic has patch breast pockets with single point flaps, rectangular flaps to the hip pockets all being fastened with brass buttons. The cuffs are fastened with three small brass buttons. A bronze 'Bays' badge is worn on each lapel. The 'Sam Browne' has a whistle on the cross strap. The dark blue forage cap is worn on parade, etc, and the khaki SD cap on other occasions.

NO. 5 DRESS, JERSEY ORDER. This, together with shirt sleeve order, is for personnel who do not normally wear overalls and consists of a black pullover for WOs and sergeants, and the issue one for ranks below. No. 2 Dress trousers, collar, tie and beret. Brass badges of rank are worn on a leather strap

The band of the 1st Queen's Dragoon Guards.

around the right wrist. The Provost wears this, or shirt sleeve order, with the forage cap.

NO. 8 DRESS, COMBAT KIT. Standard kit with sewn-on rank badge. Black webbing. The pistol and ammunition pouch, when worn, are also black.

NO. 12 DRESS, OVERALLS. As described elsewhere.

NO. 13 DRESS, SHIRT SLEEVE ORDER. Again this form of dress is described elsewhere. The stable belt is blue with the buckles at the left hip.

NO. 14 DRESS. PT kit.

The Royal Scots Greys (The 2nd Dragoons)

NO. 1 DRESS: BLUE.

FACING COLOUR: BLUE.

AMALGAMATION:

2ND JULY 1971

WITH THE 3RD

CARABINIERS AND

NOW DEFUNCT.

FULL DRESS (SOLDIERS'). See plate, page 37. A white waist belt with a brass buckle bearing the Thistle badge. Dark blue overalls with a wide yellow stripe down the sides and, when mounted, black knee boots with a knotched top. A black bearskin cap with brass chin chains, a white cut feather plume on the left side held in place by a brass grenade bearing the Royal Arms, St. Andrew's Cross and scroll reading 'WATERLOO'. On the back of the bearskin is a white metal 'HORSE OF HANOVER'. This dates from 1768 when a Royal Warrant decreed that the grenadier cap used throughout the army should have a bearskin front. The regiment was somewhat slow in adopting the new regulation, but, in 1777 they were wearing the new caps with The Order of the Thistle on the front and the 'HORSE OF HANOVER' on a scarlet backing behind. The tradition has been maintained to this day but without the backing of scarlet. On each collar is a silver eagle commemorating the capture of the Imperial Eagle of the French 45th Regiment at Waterloo by Sergeant Charles Ewart. He was later given a commission by the Prince Regent. Ewart is buried on the esplanade of Edinburgh Castle. The officers' full dress uniform is similar to the above. Gold braid is substituted for yellow. A raised gold thread grenade on a blue patch is worn on each side of the collar in place of the eagle. The cartouche belt is of gold regimental lace, as is the waistbelt, with a gilt cartouche, buckles and slides. The waistbelt buckle bears the Order of the Thistle badge and is also of gilt. The bearskin is as the soldiers' but larger and with no White Horse badge. The 1912 pattern sword is carried.

NO. 1 DRESS (SOLDIERS). See plate, page 37. White waist belt with brass buckle plate with silver 'Thistle' badge. Spurs, when worn, are the steel swans-necked type. The forage cap is dark blue with a white vandyked band of twelve points, brass side buttons and the regimental badge in silver. Throughout the book, badges, buttons and beltplates are referred to as silver or brass. In actual fact most are 'staybrite' which is more like very bright light gold or chrome, but I think it easier to use the words silver and brass. Rank stripes are of gold thread on dark blue patches. A light grey beret with silver eagle on a black rectangular patch was worn on occasions.

Regimental button.

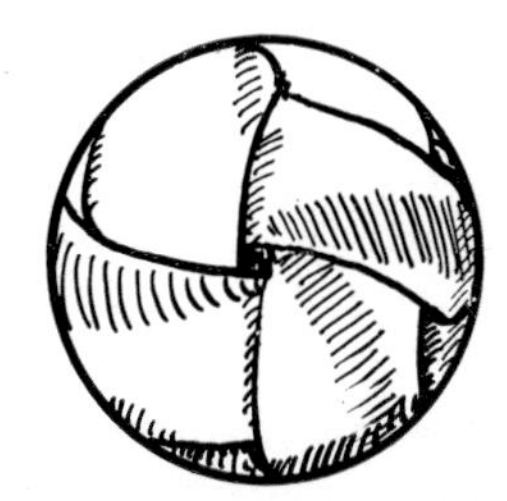

Officers' service dress button.

OFFICERS' SERVICE DRESS. Khaki with boxpleated breast pockets with three pointed flaps. Turnups to the trousers. Officers and WOIs have woven leather buttons on the tunic. Silver eagles with the heads facing inwards, on dark blue patches on the upper lapels. Brown 'Sam Browne' belt. The dark blue forage cap is piped with white around the brim and has a white vandyked band of twenty points. The chin strap buttons are brass with the 'Thistle' insignia. Silver cap badge on dark blue patch. Officers and WOIs carry a whip.

NO. 2 DRESS (SOLDIERS). Khaki issue with brass buttons and shoulder titles which reads 'GREYS'. On each lapel silver eagles, on blue patches. The eagles have no motto underneath, just the honour 'Waterloo'. White nylon web waist belt with brass buckle plate with the silver 'Thistle' badge. A white lanyard at the left shoulder. Forage cap or the grey beret, which commemorates the regiment's grey horses.

BARRACK DRESS. Officers and NCOs—light grey vee-necked pullover with sewn on badges of rank. Other ranks—khaki issue. No. 2 Dress trousers, black shoes, grey beret.

SHIRT SLEEVE ORDER. Standard issue. The stable belt is striped grey, dark blue, narrow red, narrow yellow, dark blue and grey. Buckles are worn to the front. Standard issue coveralls, etc, worn with the grey beret and on occasions a grey cravat.

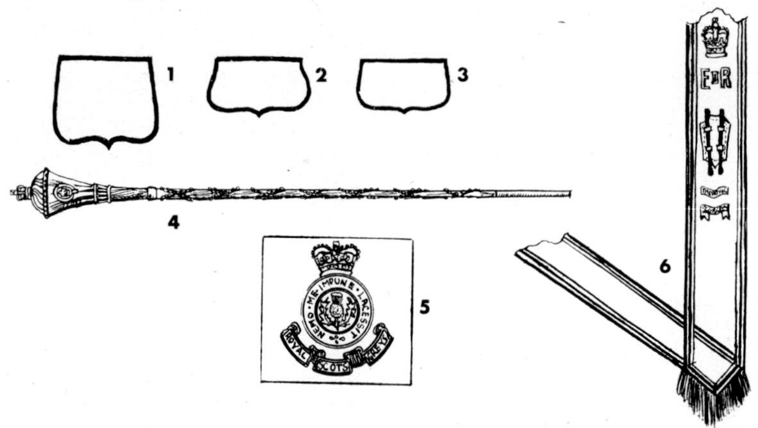

1. *Shape of Bandman's pouch,* **2.** *Drum-master's pouch,* **3.** *Soldier's pouch (RSDG),* **4.** *Drum Major's mace. Gold fittings on oak,* **5.** *Drum Major's belt plate. Brass,* **6.** *Drum Major's sash. Red, two gold braids round edge. Crown—proper colours, cypher—gold, drumsticks ($5\frac{1}{2}$ inches)—ebony on brass shield, 'Royal Scots Greys' in gold on blue, gold fringe.*

BANDSMEN. Full Dress. The uniform is basically as already described but with the addition of gold aiguilettes from the left shoulder and a red plume on the bearskin, starting from the grenade, going over the top of the cap and terminating about half way down the right side. The bass-drummer wears the famous white bearskin which also has the red plume. This was originally worn by the kettle-drummer but the band is no longer mounted. (The band bearskins are still worn by the Royal Scots Dragoon Guards but with changes in the full dress, covered in the chapter on that regiment.) It is a popular myth that the white bearskin was presented to the regiment by the Czar of Russia when he was Colonel-in-Chief, but in reality it was first worn about five years before his appointment, in about 1889. It was virtually out of use until the coronation of King George VI in 1937, when it was re-introduced. Another distinction is that the bandsmen's forage cap has a yellow vandyke band instead of a white one and, in place of the eagle badge, they wear a grenade. This is a reminder of the drummers of the early 18th century who were dressed like mounted grenadiers and wore this badge on their grenadier caps. The trumpet is silver and the banner dark blue and the arms of Scotland worked in gold and proper colours.

THE PIPES AND DRUMS. The first official Royal Scots Greys pipe band was formed in 1946. King George VI, who was very interested in pipe bands, granted the privilege of wearing the Royal Stuart tartan and also designed much of the uniform. The kilt and plaid are Royal Stuart tartan. The doublet is dark blue with silver piping for pipe majors and white for pipes. The sporran is of grey horse hair with long tassels of black and red hair, and silver mounting with the eagle badge in the centre. The bonnet is the traditional black feather one with a white vandyke band and a white feather plume issuing from a silver eagle. The plaid brooch is silver with a white 'Horse of Hanover'. Black boots, white gaiters and red and green diamond diced socks with yellow flashes. Black waist and cross belts with silver buckles, slides and chapes. The Pipe Major's pipes have a light blue velvet bag and two ribbons on the drones, one of tartan and one of blue velvet. Pipes of pipers are Royal Stuart tartan and have only one tartan ribbon on the drones. Drummers wear the regimental scarlet tunic and blue overalls. They are not classed as bandsmen and wear the white plume on their bearskins. In No. 1 blue dress and No. 2 khaki dress they wear trews of Dalyell tartan and, instead of forage caps, an Atholl bonnet with a white vandyke band and a red toorie or pompom.

The Royal Scots Dragoon Guards

(CARABINIERS AND GREYS)

NO. 1 DRESS: BLUE.

FACING COLOUR: YELLOW.

AMALGAMATION: 2ND JULY 1971—THE ROYAL SCOTS GREYS (2ND DRAGOONS) AND 3RD CARABINIERS (THE PRINCE OF WALES'S DRAGOON GUARDS)

FULL DRESS. See plate, page 37. Heavy cavalry traditionally have one stripe down the overalls, but, with the amalgamation with the 3rd Carabiniers, who were reclassified as light cavalry in 1851, the new regiment has taken on this distinction. Black bearskin cap with brass chin chains and a large brass grenade, embossed with the Royal Coat of Arms, serving as a holder for a white cut feather plume. On the back of the bearskin there is worn a white

Saladin of the RSDG. The badge is The Order of the Thistle superimposed over crossed carbines.

metal 'Horse of Hanover' badge, about $2\frac{1}{2}$ inches long. A white cross belt with a black pouch with the regimental badge on the flap. A white waist belt with a brass snake clasp. Black boots with white metal swans-neck spurs. A silver wire Waterloo Eagle is worn on either collar and, corporals and above, wear one above their rank stripes, which are gold on a yellow patch. All ranks wear a silver wire Prince of Wales's Feathers on the left upper arm. The 1908 pattern cavalry sword is carried by other ranks on white slings from the waist belt. White sword knot. Dismounted parade right markers carry a lance with a red over white pennant. The officers' full dress is basically the same with a few exceptions. Gold braid is substituted for yellow. The shoulder straps are plaited gold cord. A gold grenade is set at an angle on each side of the collar. A larger and better quality bearskin and a larger white cut feather plume are worn. Officers ceased wearing the White Horse on the back of the cap in the first half of the last century. The cross belt and waist belt are of woven gold thread with a silver pouch and gold buckles. The sword, when carried, is the 1912 officers' cavalry pattern, which is similar to the troopers' 1908 type but with a decorated steel bowl guard. There are two scabbards for this pattern of sword, one of pigskin for wearing with service dress, and one of steel for full or No. 1 dress. When mounted, the officers' chargers have a red and black horsehair throat plume, thistle stirrup runners and the Order of the Thistle on bits and breast plates. The black lambskin saddle cover has yellow scalloped edging.

NO. 1 DRESS. Standard issue blue tunic, five brass buttons stamped with a thistle. Steel shoulder chains. Corporals and above wear a woven silver wire eagle above stripes, which are gold thistle patterned on yellow felt. All ranks wear a silver wire Prince of Wales's Feathers badge on left upper arm. White woven nylon waist belt with a brass buckle on which is a silver thistle.

Pipe Major Pryde with two bandsmen. The bass drum is dark blue and yellow with red and yellow scrolls and the Royal Arms of Scotland. The side drum bears the badge of The Order of the Thistle.

The Eagle and Crossed Carbines badge on a dark blue patch is worn on either side of the collar and on the forage cap which has a yellow vandyke band of twelve points. The overalls are also blue with double yellow stripes down the sides.

OFFICERS' SERVICE DRESS. Khaki with box pleated breast pockets and three pointed flaps, rectangular horizontal flaps to side pockets. Woven brown leather buttons on all pockets, shoulder straps and down the front. Prince of Wales's Feathers badge on dark blue patch on left upper arm and Regimental badges on dark blue patches on each lapel. A wide dark brown leather cross belt with silver whistle on a strap and pouch over the left shoulder. The belt has a brass buckle and tip and the pouch has a brass Crossed Carbines and Eagle badge. The forage cap is dark blue with yellow piping around the brim and a vandyke band of twenty points. The badge is of silver and gilt on a dark blue patch. The trousers have turn-ups and brown shoes are worn. The 1912 pattern sword, in brown scabbard, slings and sword knot, suspended from under the skirt of the tunic.

NO. 2 DRESS (SOLDIERS). Standard issue, no belt, with silver wire Eagle above rank stripes for corporal and above. All ranks wear Prince of Wales's Feathers in white on left arm and bi-metal collar badges, all of which are on dark blue patches. All ranks up to WO II wear a brown leather cross belt similar to officers but slightly narrower, no whistle and lighter brown. Headwear is the forage cap previously described or a dark blue issue beret. A white lanyard is worn around left shoulder. Brass shoulder titles.

BARRACK DRESS (OFFICERS). Standard khaki/green pullover with denim patches. Service dress hat of khaki with black piping around brim, a black patch behind badge and small brass Thistle pattern buttons at the side. Badges of rank on stiff khaki worsted shoulder boards. Same dress for soldiers except for hat.

SHIRT SLEEVE ORDER. Standard. Stable belt, striped, with the order of colours from the top being wide dark blue, narrow grey, yellow, red and white dark blue. Buckles are worn to the front. All other working uniform is the same as other regiments in the armoured corps.

BANDSMEN. Basically the same as the band uniform of the 'Greys', although the facing colour is yellow. The black bearskin with the red plume extending over the top is retained, as is the white one of the kettle-drummer, but nowadays, as he is normally dismounted, this is worn by the bass-drummer of the band. The yellow vandyked forage cap with the grenade badge has also been kept. The main difference is that the heavy cavalry pattern aiguilette, which is worn on the left shoulder, has been replaced by one worn on the right and has a cord passing across the back and attached to the left shoulder. This originates from the light calavry uniform of the carabiniers.

THE PIPES AND DRUMS. Again this is similar to the Royal Scots Greys uniform with yellow instead of white for the vandyking and piping. The Eagle and Crossed Carbines badge is worn on the sporran and plume clasp. The Atholl bonnet has a yellow vandyke band. No. 1 and No. 2 dress troopers' jackets are worn with Dalyell tartan trews.

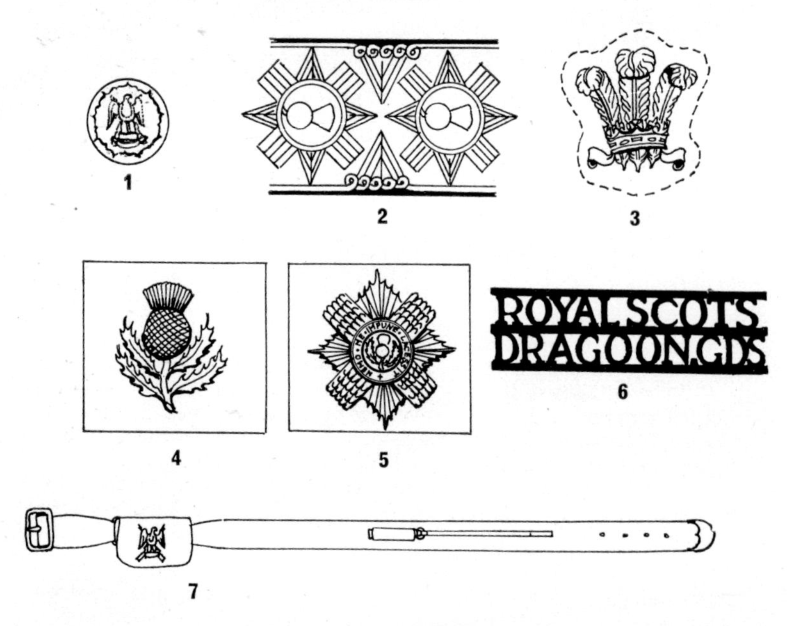

1. *Royal Scots Dragoon Guards button.* **2.** *Lace pattern of officers' full dress belts, etc, all gold with dark blue edge (RSG and RSDG).* **3.** *Prince of Wales's Feathers badge.* **4.** *Other ranks' belt buckle, silver thistle on brass.* **5.** *Officers' full dress gilt belt badge (RSG and RSDG).* **6.** *Shoulder titles in brass.* **7.** *Officers' leather cross belt. That of other ranks is similar, but has no whistle.*

3rd Carabiniers

(PRINCE OF WALES'S DRAGOON GUARDS)
NO. 1 DRESS: BLUE.
FACING COLOUR: YELLOW.
AMALGAMATION: 2ND JULY 1971— WITH THE ROYAL SCOTS GREYS

Colour party of the Carabiniers at the laying-up of their standard at Chester Cathedral. May 1972 (The Daily Telegraph).

FULL DRESS. The 6th Dragoon Guards (Carabiniers) (the regiment is an amalgamation of the aforementioned and the 3rd [POW] Dragoon Guards) was converted to light cavalry in the 19th century, but retained their title of 'Dragoons'. The helmet is brass with a silver star and '3' within a garter. The plume is black and red. The pouch on the crossbelt is black leather with the Carabinier's badge on the centre of the flap.

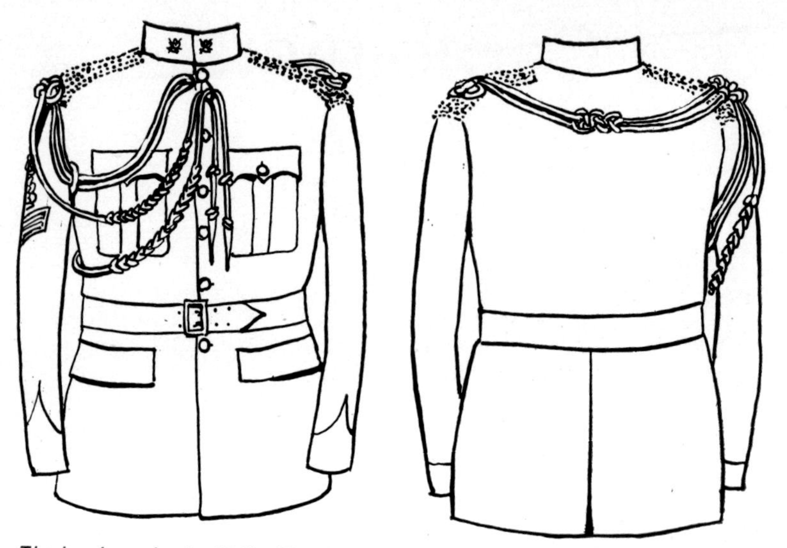

The bandsman's aiguillette. The distinction has been adopted by the band of the Royal Scots Drogoon Guards.

No. 1 Dress arm badge (3½ inches high). Made of metal thread and sequins on a yellow patch. The feathers are silver and the carbines and crown are gold. The motto is gold on blue silk.

Officers' long dark blue coat sometimes worn with Mess or No. 1 Dress. The underside of the collar is yellow and the coat is lined in white. Just showing under the collar is a gilt throat chain with lion's head fasteners.

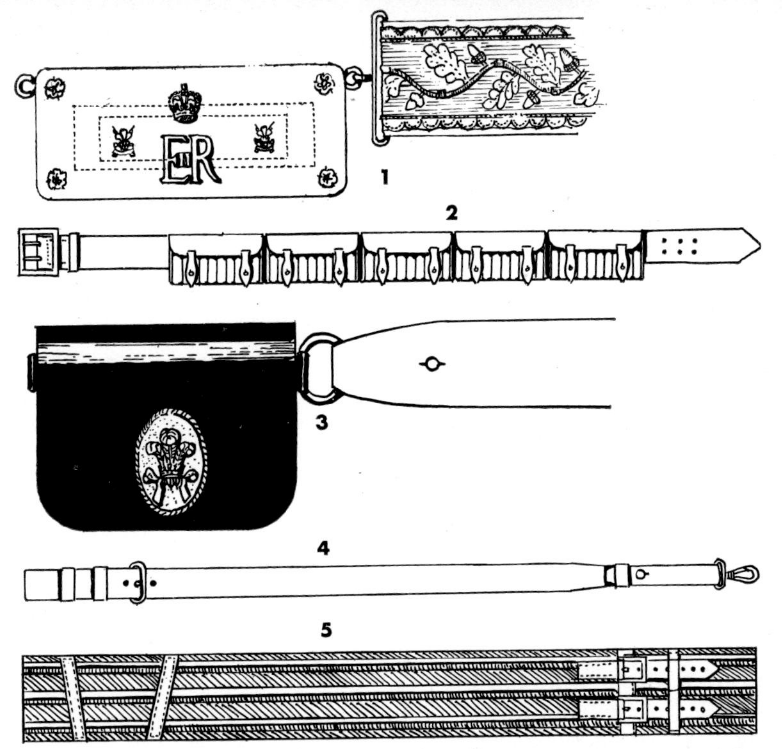

1. *Officers, the RSM and Bandmaster. No. 1 Dress pouch and belt.* **2.** *Bandolier in brown leather with brass fittings worn by the Orderly Warrant Officer. The original dates from the Boer War. Orderlies also carry a straw coloured whip with silver mounts.* **3.** *Pouch and belt worn on occasions by the COs orderly and Orderly NCOs. The badge is the No. 2 Dress arm badge.* **4.** *The 'Sam Browne' cross strap. The buckle is worn at the back.* **5.** *Stable belt. The diagonal leather pieces are worn on the right.*

NO. 1 DRESS. Officers, the RSM and the Bandmaster: The tunic is not waisted and there are no buttons on the pockets or the sleeves. The sleeve cuffs are plain and the pocket flaps are three-pointed. Silver and gilt collar badges, shoulder chains and brass buttons down the front. The crossbelt is of oakleaf and acorn gold lace with white edging, suspended from which is a rectangular silver pouch. The belt has gilt fittings but no chains and pickers. The overalls have two $\frac{3}{4}$ inch white stripes $\frac{1}{4}$ inch apart. The forage cap for all ranks is blue with a yellow band. All officers (except RSM and Bandmaster) wear field officer's gold braid on the peak.

All other ranks wear the blue serge issue which has the normal configuration of buttons, which are brass and bear the same device as the badge. The arm badge is worn the same as other regiments and the gold chevrons are shown on a yellow backing. The Warrant Officer's badges have yellow backings also. The band wear a unique form of aiguillette. They are of pale yellow silken cord, with gilt tags which are the same as those worn by officers of the Household Cavalry. They are suspended from the right shoulder, a distinction normally only accorded to officers. They differ further in that they are extended from the right shoulder, across the back and terminate in a trefoil fixed to the chainmail on the left shoulder.

OFFICERS' SERVICE DRESS. Plain patch pockets with rounded flaps to the breast pockets and rectangular flaps to those on the hips. Officers wear rank badges, but no titles, on the shoulder straps. The collar badges on the lapels are the Regimental badge which has silver POW feathers with gold carbines, coronet, motto and scroll. Forage cap, or, when off duty, the side hat which has a yellow top and dark blue bottom half, bound with gold lace. The 'Sam Browne' is a special regimental pattern.

NO. 2 DRESS, SOLDIERS. Brass buttons, 3DG shoulder titles, collar badges and a white woven lanyard around the left shoulder. A brown 'patent' plastic waist belt with a brass plate and the Carabinier's badge in the centre. Forage cap or side hat. The Regimental arm badge in this order of dress is a 2 inch white metal oval with a brass coronet. Corporals carry a whip.

COMBAT DRESS, ETC. The stable belt is, from the top, blue/white/yellow/red repeated four times and ending in blue. The buckles are on the left side. The badge on the officers' beret is embroidered. In 1962 the helmet and webbing were black but whether this continued until the amalgamation I am unable to say. The Provost Sergeant wears a 'Sam Browne' belt but with the cross belt hanging down on the left hip, rather in the manner of the Household Cavalry's joined sword slings. No armlet is worn.

4th/7th Royal Dragoon Guards

NO. 1 DRESS: BLUE.

FACING COLOUR: BLUE.

AMALGAMATION:

APRIL 1922—4TH ROYAL IRISH DRAGOON GUARDS AND 7TH DRAGOON GUARDS (PRINCESS ROYAL'S) TO FORM 4TH/7TH DRAGOON GUARDS.

REDESIGNATED:

OCTOBER 1936—4TH/7TH ROYAL DRAGOON GUARDS.

FULL DRESS. See plate, page 48. Wellington boots—worn under the overalls when dismounted—swan's neck spurs and white gauntlets. The helmet is of the dragoon type in brass with the badge in silver and a white horsehair plume. The officers' helmet has black horsehair on top and white underneath. The lance, carried by parade markers, etc, has a pennant with blue at the top, red below and a narrow strip of yellow in the middle.

The Regiment's standard and guard. The background to all detail is the same crimson as the flag. Honours, fringe, frames in the corners and the words around the Silver Star are all in gold.

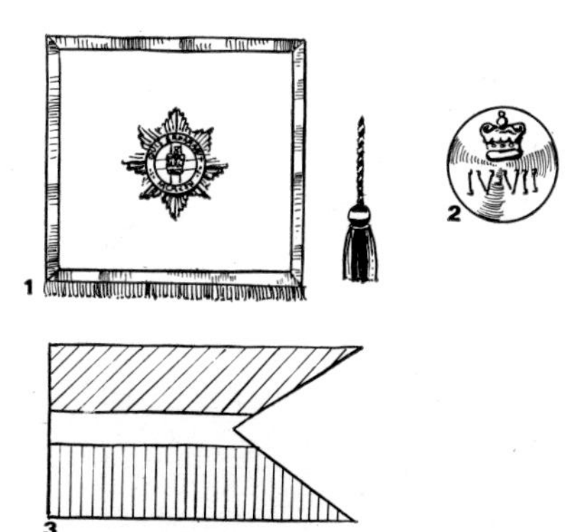

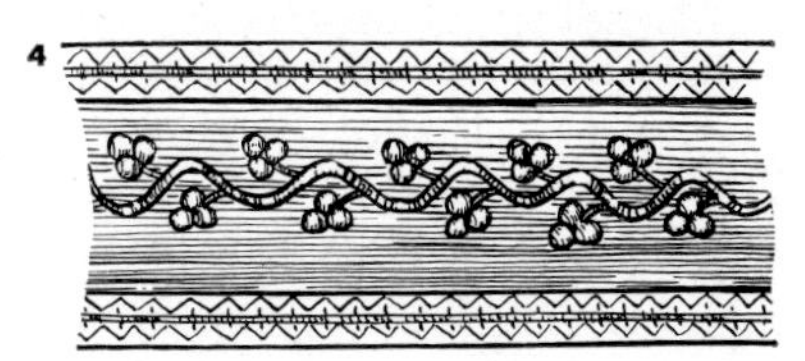

1. *Trumpet banner—dark blue velvet, silver braid fringe and star. Pale blue garter, red crown and cross on white ground with gold piping around garter, cross and base of crown. Tassels and cords blue/red/yellow.* **2.** *Regimental button,* **3.** *Lance pennant.* **4.** *Pattern of officers' gold lace for cross belts, etc. This lace is also used by the Queen's Royal Irish Hussars.*

NO. 1 DRESS. See plate, page 36. Although No. 1 dress is now really 'out', the Orderly Officer and the Orderly Sergeant Major wear it in the evening. The band and all NCOs wear it on occasions. In 1971 a half guard of approximately fifty all ranks were turned out in No. 1's. The last time it was worn by the Regiment as a whole was in 1967 at the opening of the Regimental Museum in Halifax. The Officers' No. 1 is similar to the above but it is fitted better and the hip pockets are the same pattern as those in the breast. Also the overalls are tighter. The badges are enamelled in the centre with a blue garter and red cross on a white ground. They also wear a gold lace crossbelt with a silver cartouche. The 1912 pattern sword has a gold and black striped cord sword knot. The officers' forage cap is dark blue velvet with a gold wire band around the front edge of the peak. Officially this gold braid is worn only by Majors and above (Field Officers) but it is worn by all officers of the regiment.

OFFICERS' SERVICE DRESS. Khaki with centre vent to the skirt of the jacket and rounded edges, box pleated top pockets with single pointed flaps, deep rectangular flaps to the lower pockets. It is fastened with four brass buttons down the front, two small buttons on each cuff and one on each breast pocket and shoulder strap. Silver collar badges and brass shoulder titles reading 4/7RDG. A wide crossbelt with a whistle attached by a strap. Brown toe cap shoes. A khaki SD cap or the dark blue velvet forage cap, with enamelled version of the Regimental badge.

NO. 2 DRESS (SOLDIERS). Standard issue with Regimental collar badges and brass shoulder titles reading 4/7RDG. A white lanyard around the right shoulder. A brown imitation patent leather belt with the silver star on a rect-angular brass belt-plate. Dark blue forage cap or side hat. The silver badge has a dark red, star-shaped, felt patch behind it. NCOs follow the pattern of other regiments and wear the Regimental badge above their chevrons.

The stable belt, worn with shirt sleeve order, etc, is from the top, dark red, a narrow yellow strip, dark blue. The webbing is black and the old '37 pattern is considered to be more practical for work in tanks. The regimental black cravat is worn optionally on exercise.

The badge on the upper left arm is the Regiment's colours of blue, yellow and red. The Regiment was at Dunkirk in 1940 and while there, they removed their badge from their khaki side hats. On their return to England there was difficulty in identifying to which regiment they belonged. The Adjutant, Captain J. A. D'A Goldsmith, now the Colonel of the Regiment, instigated the flash. They then joined 27th Armoured brigade together with the 13th/18th Royal Hussars and the Staffordshire Yeomanry. All three adopted flashes of their respective colours. The 13th/18th still wear their dark blue and white diamond.

NEXT PAGE: A trooper of the 4th/7th Royal Dragoon Guards on exercise. The cravat is black. The vehicle in the background is a FV438.

NUNNS

5th Royal Inniskilling Dragoon Guards

UNIFORM JACKET: BLUE.
TROUSERS: DARK GREEN.
FACING COLOUR: BLUE.
AMALGAMATION: APRIL 1922—5TH DRAGOON GUARDS (PRINCESS CHARLOTTE'S OF WALES) AND 6TH DRAGOONS (THE INNISKILLINGS) TO FORM 5TH/6TH DRAGOONS.
REDESIGNATED: MAY 1927—5TH INNISKILLING DRAGOON GUARDS JUNE 1935—5TH ROYAL INNISKILLING DRAGOON GUARDS.

FULL DRESS. This order of dress is used only on ceremonial occasions by quarter guards, bandsmen and the commanding officer's trumpeter. It is of the usual dragoon pattern. With the following distinctions. Blue collar and shoulder straps, piped in yellow, on the scarlet jacket. Blue pointed cuffs with yellow cord Austrian knots above. Nine brass buttons down the front, which is also piped. Collar and shoulder badges as No. 1 dress. White waist belt fitted with sword slings and fastened with a brass and silver buckle. A white cross-belt with a black pouch and brass buckle, which is positioned in

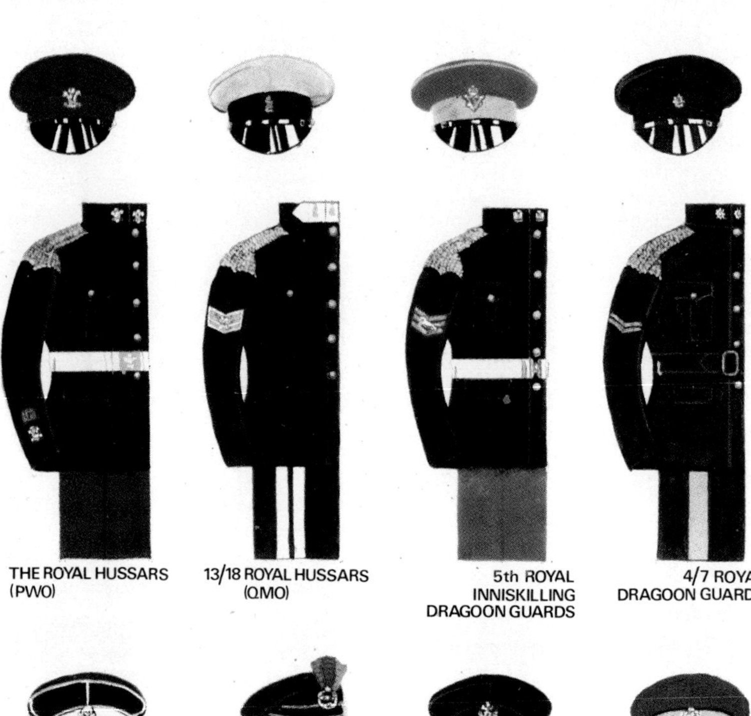

THE ROYAL HUSSARS (PWO)

13/18 ROYAL HUSSARS (QMO)

5th ROYAL INNISKILLING DRAGOON GUARDS

4/7 ROYAL DRAGOON GUARDS

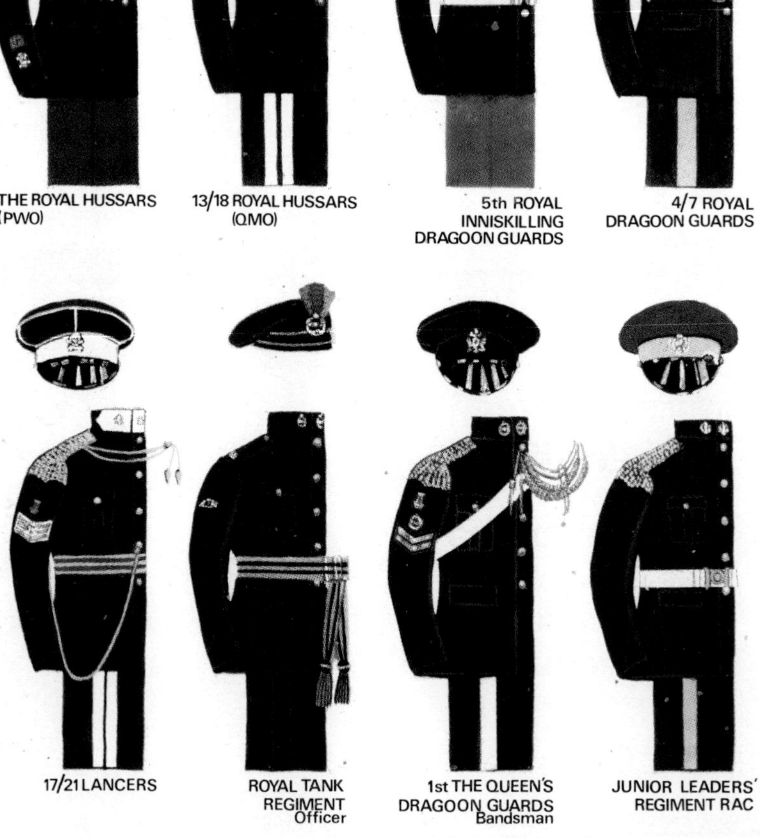

17/21 LANCERS

ROYAL TANK REGIMENT Officer

1st THE QUEEN'S DRAGOON GUARDS Bandsman

JUNIOR LEADERS' REGIMENT RAC

14/20 KING'S HUSSARS

THE QUEEN'S OWN HUSSARS

15/19 ROYAL HUSSARS

9/12 ROYAL LANCERS

THE ROYAL SCOTS GREYS

ROYAL SCOTS DRAGOON GUARDS

3rd CARABINIERS R.S.M

THE QUEEN'S ROYAL IRISH HUSSARS

front of the shoulder strap. The dragoon helmet is brass with a white and red horsehair plume. Green overalls with a single yellow stripe down each leg, black boots and steel spurs.

NO. 1 DRESS. Dark blue tunic, brass buttons, shoulder chainmail and Inniskilling Castle collar badges with the flags flying outwards. Rank chevrons are gold on a red patch, and senior NCOs wear a silver 'Horse of Hanover' on a green patch under their rank badge on the lower right sleeve. Officers and senior non-commissioned officers wear a cross belt and pouch. Gold lace for officers and the RSM and the white leather full dress type for the other senior NCOs. Junior ranks have a white nylon waist belt, fastened with a 1937 pattern webbing clips and runners. All wear green trousers and black shoes. Officers and WOs have a yellow stripe down the sides. The forage cap is also green, with a buff coloured hatband and piping around the brim. (I believe it is called primrose in the regiment, but buff is a truer description.) The Regimental badge is silver with a green patch behind it. The buckle on the chinstrap is on the right. All other regiments wear this on the left.

The Commanding Officer's guard wear green trousers with a yellow stripe, white gloves and carry a Stirling SMG.

Commanding Officer's trumpeter in Full Dress.

No. 1 Dress. Left to Right, Officer, troopers, and colour party comprised of senior NCOs.

NO. 2 DRESS. Khaki tunic with brass buttons, which are all the same size. Collar badges as for No. 1 Dress. Shoulder titles have the initials 5DG with the Castle badge above, the flags flying to the rear. A white lanyard is worn around the left shoulder. In second best No. 2 dress, the khaki cloth belt is worn, and in parade order, the white web belt described above. Parade order is normally worn on all regimental ceremonial parades, for regimental office and main gate guard duty. The duty trumpeter wears a white crossbelt. The green trousers are also worn with this order with green socks and black shoes or boots. The No. 1 dress hat, or side hat, which has a green lower half piped in buff, buff top and brass buttons is worn with second best No. 2 dress. Senior NCOs wear the 'Horse' badge previously described.

OFFICERS' SERVICE DRESS. The tunic is of the regimental cut with a four button fastening down the front, buttons on the breast pockets and shoulder straps and three on each cuff. The cavalry 'Sam Browne' belt, with a

The Regiment's trumpeters. Note that they are wearing Household Cavalry type sword belts with the slings buckled together. The woollen aiguillettes are yellow with brass tips.

whistle, green trousers and the regimental pattern forage cap with gold braid on the peak are worn. Black shoes and socks.

BEST SHIRT SLEEVE ORDER. Forage cap, No. 2 dress shirt, green trousers, white belt and shoes.

SECOND BEST SHIRT SLEEVE ORDER. Forage cap, side hat or beret, shirt, khaki trousers, stable belt and boots.

BARRACK DRESS. Beret or side hat, shirt and tie, issue pullover. Officers, WOs, S/sergeants and sergeants wear a green vee-necked pullover with badges of rank on the right arm. The regimental stable belt is worn over the pullover with khaki trousers and black boots or shoes.

Only officers and warrant officers wear green trousers with this order of dress.

DRESS FOR TRAINING. Combat suit, khaki flannel shirt and tie or dark green scarf, beret, boots and black web belt and gaiters.

AFV crews wear coveralls, khaki flannel shirt and tie or dark green scarf, beret, boots and black webbing.

1. *Collar badge, the flags flying outwards. Brass motto, silver castle.* **2.** *Regimental button in brass.* **3.** *Stable belt: red, green, yellow.*

LEFT to RIGHT. Corporal, The Royal Hussars. 2/Lt The Queen's Own Hussars (Hong Kong). Officer. DPM Combat dress. Corporal, Royal Scots Dragoon Guards. Polo Kit, 14/20 Royal Hussars. Sergeant, The Queen's Royal Irish Hussars.

1. Life Guard helmet. 2. Trumpet banner of the Household Cavalry. 3. Life Guard tunic. 4. Back of soldier's tunic. 5. Cuirass. 6. Household Cavalry pouch and belt. 7. Life Guard Musician's collar. 8. Soldier's sword and belt. 9. Jack boot. 10. Blues and Royals helmet. 11. Blues and Royals tunic (trooper). 12. Back of soldier's tunic. 13. Forage cap. 14. Back of officer's tunic, officer's aiguilettes and cuff. 15. Gauntlet. 16. Blues and Royals Musician's cuff. 17. Musician's shoulder strap. Next to the Blues and Royals helmet is the collar of the Blues and Royals Musicians, which has a different lace pattern to that of the Life Guards.

The Queen's Own Hussars

NO. 1 DRESS: BLUE.
FACING COLOUR: GARTER BLUE.
AMALGAMATION: 3RD NOVEMBER 1958—3RD THE QUEEN'S OWN HUSSARS AND 7TH THE QUEEN'S OWN HUSSARS.

The regimental drum horse 'Crusader' who was presented to the regiment by HRH Princess Margaret in 1958. The QOH is the only cavalry regiment of the line that still retains a kettle drummer and horse. The silver drums in the picture were captured at Dettingen in 1743, and are inscribed with regimental battle honours. The drum horse leads the band on all ceremonial parades. The kettle drummer, in addition to the full dress, wears a 3 inches high silver collar.

Guidon bearer and escort in No. 1 dress.

Officers' tropical dress, light khaki/sand drill, brown buttons, shoes and cross belt, scarlet side hat or forage cap. Officers' side hat and beret badge: Blue garter, red centre, gold wire around garter and crown, silver wire horse and cypher.

FULL DRESS (SOLDIERS). See plate, page 37. The regimental cypher is worn on each side of the collar and on the flap of the pouch. It is also worn on the arm above rank stripes, worked in silver wire on Garter Blue patch, but in this case it is without the motto and is 2½ inches high. The sword, when carried, is the 1908 cavalry pattern worn on white leather sling from under the skirt of the jacket. White sword knot.

NO. 1 DRESS. Worn by all Officers, Warrant Officers, Senior and Junior NCOs on regimental duties or ceremonial duties. Standard issue blue tunic with scarlet collar. Half dome plain brass buttons. No waist belt (a white cavalry

Detail of combat dress camouflage.

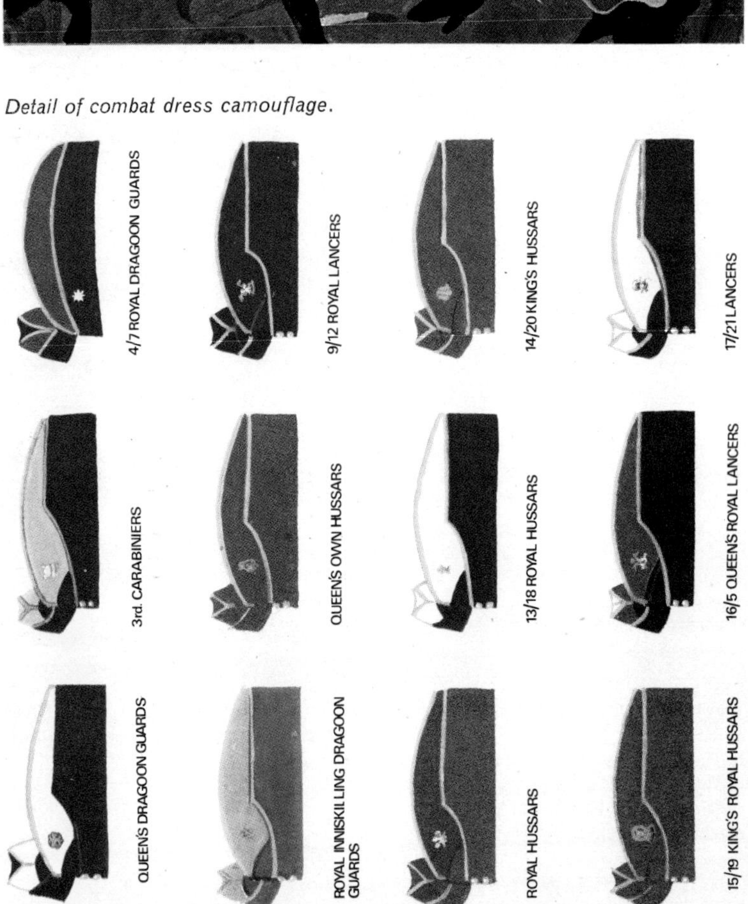

LEFT to RIGHT. Trooper in no. 1 Dress. The Blues and Royals. Corporal of Horse in no. 2 Dress (mounted). The Life Guards. Winter Guard order cloak. The Life Guards. Mounted drummer in state dress. Officer in review order (dismounted). The Blues and Royals. Officer in service Dress (mounted). The Life Guards.

Note crossbelt on the Colonel and the 'Maid of Warsaw' badges on the troopers' left lower arms.

cross belt is sometimes worn). Shoulder chains. Dark blue overalls with double yellow stripes. Black wellington boots with steel swan's-neck spurs. Scarlet forage cap with black leather chin strap, held in place by plain brass buttons. Officers wear the Regimental Crest embroidered in gold wire, with a blue garter and White Horse on red ground. Other ranks wear the White Horse with the motto in brass. Officers also wear the gold braided peak. The regimental cypher badge on each side of the collar, and above the rank stripes or below the crown, is worn by WOs. The 1912 pattern sword for officers and the 1908 pattern for other ranks is suspended by white sling from under the tunic. The swords have a white sword knot and are normally carried only by colour parties and guards of honour.

OFFICERS' SERVICE DRESS. Khaki, horizontal side pockets with buttoned flaps. Patch breast pockets (no pleats), rectangular buttoned flap. All buttons half domed plain brass. Side vents to jacket. QOH Officers wear a brown leather cross belt, not a 'Sam Browne'. Shoulder titles in brass, reading QOH. Maid of Warsaw badge on left lower arm. Scarlet forage cap or all khaki service dress cap. Sword, when carried, attached by long brown leather sling from under jacket.

Cypher badge of the Queen's Own Hussars (the arm badge is without the motto).

Two troopers in normal summer combat dress. Denims, boots, beret, brown web belt, Stirling SMG.

NO. 2 DRESS (SOLDIERS). Khaki standard issue, no belt. Plain half dome buttons. Brass QOH shoulder titles. Collar badges are white metal cypher with brass crown and motto on red felt patches. Scarlet forage cap with White Horse badge, or a scarlet side hat with gold piping when not on regimental duty. 'Maid of Warsaw' badge on the left forearm. This badge, which is in the form of a red shield with a white mermaid and border, was granted to the 7th Hussars (now QOH) for assistance to the 2nd Polish Corps, under General Anders, in the Italian Campaign, 15th June to 2nd September 1944.

BARRACK DRESS. Officers—SD trousers and cap, lovat green vee-neck pullover with stitched-on shoulder straps, shirt and tie. Other ranks—issue khaki pullover, forage cap or beret and No. 2 trousers.

SHIRT SLEEVE ORDER. Trousers as barrack dress, stable belt which has three equal stripes of Garter Blue, yellow, Garter Blue, each blue stripe having a thin scarlet line through the centre. The buckles are worn on the left hip. Forage or side hats.

Combat dress, overalls, etc, are standard. A Garter Blue cravat is sometimes worn on active service or on exercise.

14/20 KING'S HUSSARS

THE QUEEN'S OWN HUSSARS

9/12 ROYAL LANCERS (12th LANCERS)

THE QUEEN'S ROYAL IRISH HUSSARS

ROYAL SCOTS GREYS up to JUNE 1971

ROYAL SCOTS DRAGOON GUARDS

13/18 ROYAL HUSSARS

TRUMPETER 4/7 ROYAL DRAGOON GUARDS

The Queen's Royal Irish Hussars

NO. 1 DRESS: BLUE.
FACING COLOUR: EMERALD GREEN.
AMALGAMATION: 24TH OCTOBER 1958—4TH THE QUEEN'S OWN HUSSARS AND 8TH THE KING'S ROYAL IRISH HUSSARS.

1. *Full dress, adjutants and orderly officers' cross belt—gold and red with silver chains and pickers.*
2. *Gold lace cross belt on red leather worn with No. 1 Dress. Only the Commanding Officer and adjutant wear the Sovereign's cypher on their cartouche.*

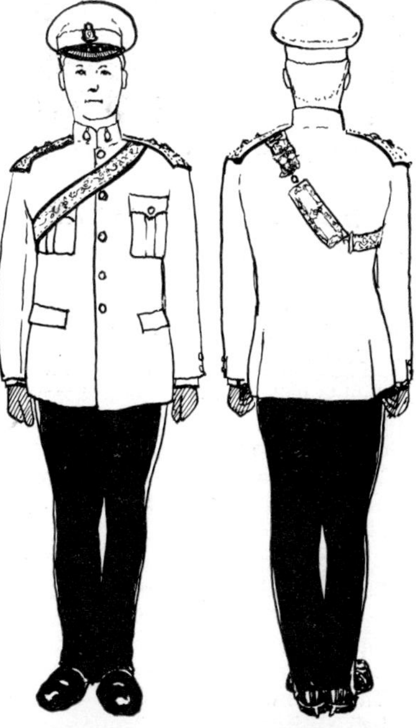

No. 3 Dress—tropical patrols. The same cut as No. 1 Dress—blue patrols except that the jacket is white drill and there is a green underlay to the shoulder chains.

FULL DRESS. See plate, page 48. NCOs have gold chevrons with the 'Harp' arm badge above, on the right arm only. The Harp is taken from the badge of the 8th Hussars who were also nicknamed the 'Crossbelt Dragoons'. The 8th were first on active service at Almenara, Spain in 1710. They pursued and cut down a Spanish cavalry corps with swords from captured Spanish crossbelts. Crossbelts were worn by the 8th as a distinction for many years after. The present regiment still bears the nickname and wear a white diagonal cross on their polo shirts.

Note the bands around the berets which are green. The rest of the beret is of the normal dark blue.

Sir Winston Churchill, his son and grandson were all in the King's Royal Irish Hussars, and Sir Winston was Colonel-in-Chief of the regiment from after the war until his death.

NO. 1 DRESS. This follows the normal pattern, with an all blue uniform and double yellow stripes on the trousers or overalls. The buttons are brass full ball type and are all the same size. Chains on the shoulders and collar badges complete the tunic. Officers wear a gold crossbelt and the band a white one. The dress hat is scarlet and the badge is a silver harp in a gold circle with motto. In the case of officers it is embroidered gold and silver wire on a dark blue patch.

OFFICERS' SERVICE DRESS. The tunic has single pointed flaps on the breast pockets and horizontal rectangular flaps to the hip pockets. All four are buttoned. There are also two buttons on the cuffs plus the normal four down the front and one on each shoulder strap. All buttons are ¾ inch plain brass ball in shape. The collar badges are brass with silver harps, facing inwards. There are no shoulder titles and the rank badges are in cloth. There is no waist belt. QRIH officers wear a brown leather pouch belt with chains and pickers in brass, as are the belt buckles etc. The pouch is engraved silver with a gilt badge in the centre. Apart from the normal SD cap they also wear what is called a 'tent hat' for obvious reasons. It is dark green with gold braid and piping. The origins of this headwear are a little obscure. It seems that it was introduced in 1909 by Lt Col H. F. Deare and was initially also worn with mess dress. Officers on manoeuvres always wore it in the evening with service dress instead of mess dress. When the War Office tried to standardise the uniforms of the RAC after World War 2 it was told that the tent hat was a reminder of the head-dress worn by the regiment during winter in the Crimea and that the gold lace represented the flap of the woollen cap (Balaclava helmet).

NO. 2 DRESS. Standard. Collar badges and brass ball buttons as described for service dress. The khaki cloth belt is not worn. The Regimental green belt, which is 1937 pattern webbing painted green and with a brass plate with a silver harp on it, is worn with best drill order.

Best drill order is worn on the following occasions: Ceremonial parades and Guards of Honour; Commanding Officer's Parade (CO's orders/interviews); Formal or social duties; Garrison duties; Regimental Police. In addition QRIH titles are worn on each shoulder strap and around the right arm is a yellow lanyard. Lance Corporals of this regiment wear two chevrons instead of one, and corporals and above have the regiment's harp arm badge above the chevrons. The No. 1 dress hat is worn on duty and the side hat, which is green with yellow piping, can be worn on informal occasions.

DAY TO DAY DRESS. This covers 1 pullover order and 2 shirt sleeve order.
Officers and Warrant Officers. **1.** SD cap. Green v-necked jersey with cloth rank badges. Shirt, tie and brown shoes. No. 2 trousers. **2.** Cotton open-necked shirt, No. 2 trousers, stable belt. (From top—green, narrow yellow and blue, green). Brown shoes.
SQMS, S/Sergeants and Sergeants. **1.** Dark blue beret with a wide green head-band, green jersey with chevrons sewn on right sleeve, shirt and tie, trousers and boots. **2.** Beret, cotton shirt with white rank chevrons on right sleeve and brass QRIH on the shoulder straps. Trousers, stable belt and boots.
Corporals and below. **1.** Beret with green band, issue pullover, chevrons on right sleeve with stable belt worn over the pullover. Flannel shirt, trousers and black boots. **2.** Beret, open-necked khaki flannel shirt, rank badges and shoulder titles. Stable belt, trousers and boots.

COMBAT DRESS, ETC. These forms of dress follow the standard pattern. A bottle green cravat is sometimes worn during training or on exercise. Officers also wear the beret with the green band, but in their case it is 1 inch wide silk.
An interesting tradition of this regiment is the 'green suit'. It is made of serge material in the cavalry manner, that is: double breasted and side vents. The front has six gilt buttons engraved with the cypher and there are also three on each cuff. White soft collar shirt, black bow tie and black shoes. The suit is worn by Officers at Mess Supper Nights.

1. *Cypher badge of the Queen's Royal Irish Hussars worn by officers on their berets and silver cartouches, on the first in gold wire and on the second in gilt.*

Officer in tent hat and pouch belt.

9th/12th Royal Lancers

NO. 1 DRESS: BLUE.
FACING COLOUR: SCARLET.
AMALGAMATION: 11TH SEPTEMBER 1960: 9TH THE QUEEN'S ROYAL LANCERS AND 12TH ROYAL LANCERS (PRINCE OF WALES).

FULL DRESS *12th Lancers*. See plate, page 48. White cartouche belt with brass fittings and black pouch with silver Prince of Wales feathers. White gauntlets with polished cuffs. Dark blue overalls with double yellow stripes. Black boots with steel spurs. Full dress is normally worn only by parade markers on ceremonial occasions. They carry a bamboo lance with a red over white pennant.
9th Lancers. Both uniforms are used by the Regiment. See plate, page 33. Senior ranks have gold braid around the collar and cuffs and, in addition to the caplines across the chest, a white crossbelt from the left shoulder.

NO. 1 DRESS. *Officers and RSM:* Dark blue tunics of the standard cut with red piping down the back seam of the sleeves and down the seams of the back, similar to that on the lance tunic. The collar is red and collar badges are not worn. Brass titles are worn instead on the shoulder chain mail. Gold crossbelt with silver pouch, chains, pickers and fittings. Scarlet forage cap (dress hat) piped around the crown, the hat band and at the quarters with dark blue, (in memory of the lance cap) black peak with gold braid band for officers. Embroidered badge. Dark blue overalls with double yellow stripes. Swan's neck spurs.
Other ranks: Dark blue tunic with red gorget patches, which have rounded rear edges, on the collar. Collar badges are the same as the cap badge, which is in brass with the feathers and the bottom half of the lance pennons in silver. The shoulder chains have no titles on them. White waist belt with brass plate. Bandsmen wear a white crossbelt from the left shoulder with caplines (as Full Dress) from the right. The end of the line, normally hooked to the lance cap, is fastened to the chainmail on the right shoulder. The regimental arm badge, which is the Prince of Wales' feathers, is worn on the right arm over rank stripes or under warrant badges. Overalls and trousers are as above, as is the forage cap but with a metal badge. No. 1 dress is issued only to corporals and above. Parade markers and quarter guards (ceremonial guards formed for visiting General Officers, etc) carry lances.

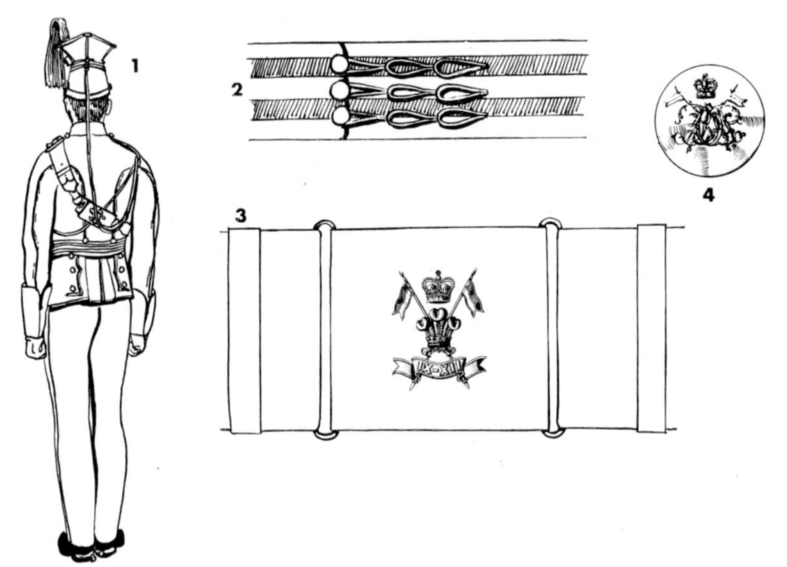

1. *Rear view of full dress 12th Lancers.* **2.** *Detail of waist belt fastening. Loops are yellow.* **3.** *Belt plate (No. 1 and No. 2 Dress).* **4.** *Button.*

Ceremonial banner of the Commanding Officer's trumpeter. It has gold portcullises and wheatsheaves on blue. The Tudor roses are red and white. The banner is the arms of the 4th Duke of Westminster who was Colonel of the Regiment from 1961–1967. BELOW: The arm badge which is silver, approximately 2½″ high, on a scarlet patch.

Combat Dress. A dark green/khaki anorak-type top which zips and buttons down the front. It also buttons at the cuff and on the pockets. Note name tab on left chest in black on dark green. The combat trousers have padded knees and are of a brown khaki colour. Khaki woollen gloves or mittens.

OFFICERS' SERVICE DRESS. Box pleated breast pockets with three pointed flaps. All four pockets are buttoned and there are also two small buttons on each cuff. Collar badges but no shoulder titles. Brown 'Sam Browne' belt and gloves. Scarlet forage cap, all khaki SD cap with bronze badge, or side hat, which for officers is dark blue with gold piping and an embroidered badge.

NO. 2 DRESS. Khaki issue, brass buttons, collar badges, white waist belt and a red/yellow/red plaited lanyard around the left shoulder. Scarlet forage cap with blue piping. The other ranks' side hat is scarlet piped in yellow, for informal use only. The regiment's arm badge is also worn with this order of dress by corporals and above.

A typical list of uniforms required by an Officer (in this case the 9th/12th Royal Lancers), is as follows:

		No. required
1.	Service dress	1
2.	SD trousers for shirt sleeve order	1
3.	Sam Browne	1
4.	Sword frog (brown leather)	1
5.	Sword with leather and metal scabbard	1
6.	Brown shoes with toe caps	2 prs.
7.	Silk tie (crochet)	1
8.	Service dress hat	1
9.	Side hat (optional)	1
10.	Leather whip	1
11.	Unlined plain leather gloves	1 pr.
12.	Shirts (one with detachable collar)	4 minimum
13.	Fawn socks	6 prs.
14.	Blue patrol jacket	1
15.	Overalls	1
16.	Black leather Wellington boots—with box spurs	1 pr.
17.	Swan necked spurs	1 pr.
18.	No. 1 dress hat	1
19.	Gloves—white cotton	2 prs.
20.	Mess jacket and waistcoat (old-fashioned 9th or 12th mess dress allowed provided they are in good order)	1
21.	Dark blue beret with embroidered badge	1
22.	Sword slings (gold braid 9th or 12th pattern) (optional)	1
23.	Pouch belt (optional)	1
24.	British warm overcoat (optional)	1
25.	Green regimental sweater	1
26.	Riding mackintosh	1
	Combat kit, etc is supplied from stores	

COMBAT KIT. Until recently a red cravat was worn on exercise but a khaki terry towelling one is now favoured. Issue kit for all ranks.

SHIRT SLEEVE ORDER. Service dress hat or dark blue side hat for officers. Dress hat, scarlet side hat or beret for other ranks. The stable belt, with the buckles on the left hip, is red, yellow, red, yellow, red, the outside reds being very narrow and the rest of the stripes being of equal width.

The Royal Hussars

(THE PRINCE OF WALES' OWN)
UNIFORM JACKET: BLUE.
TROUSERS: CRIMSON.
FACING COLOUR: CRIMSON.
AMALGAMATION: 25TH OCTOBER 1969: 10TH ROYAL HUSSARS (PRINCE OF WALES' OWN) AND 11TH HUSSARS (PRINCE ALBERT'S OWN).

FULL DRESS. See plate, page 36. Crimson trousers were formerly worn by all ranks of the 11th Hussars (PAO). They were from the livery of Prince Albert, who gave the 11th the privilege of wearing his uniform after they had escorted him from Dover in 1840, when he came to marry Queen Victoria. Black fur busby with a red bag piped in yellow, white over red plume, brass chin chains and yellow cap lines.

NO. 1 DRESS. Dark blue jacket, chain mail on the shoulders with brass titles. 10th Hussar collar badges, gold braid chevrons on the right arm only. Lance Corporals and above wear the regimental silver Prince of Wales' feathers, on crimson backing above the chevrons or below the warrant badge. A white woven nylon belt with a brass beltplate, bearing the silver feathers badge, is being issued. Plain crimson trousers and a crimson 11th Hussar pattern forage cap with Royal Hussar cap badge. Black socks, black boots when on duty, shoes off duty and Wellington boots with spurs for special occasions. This dress is no longer officially recognised in the army, and is normally worn only when authorised by the Commanding Officer. It would appear though that most regiments use it whenever possible, as they do with Full Dress, as it is certainly a more glamorous uniform than the usual khaki. The army in the past has always been loath to do away with uniforms they prize just because of the new regulations and have been known to wear them many years later. It is part of what tradition is made of.

OFFICERS' SERVICE DRESS. The jacket is of khaki whipcord and of the cavalry pattern. No collar badges. Brass buttons and a cavalry Sam Browne with a silver whistle on the cross strap. Crimson trousers and black shoes. Off duty a crimson and scarlet side hat, piped in gold, can be worn. There is also a crimson tent hat (see Queen's Royal Irish Hussars) piped and braided with gold but without the badge. The officers forage cap has gold braid on the peak. This is normally reserved for officers of field rank.

NO. 2 DRESS. Khaki jacket, shoulder titles, no collar badges or lanyard. Cloth type chevrons with regimental badge as described in No. 1 dress. Crimson trousers for best order and khaki when working. Black socks with the crimson trousers. Crimson forage cap or side hat.

SHIRT SLEEVE ORDER. Officers, WOs and sergeants wear a khaki cotton shirt and troopers wear a khaki flannel one with the top button only unfastened. The sleeves are rolled up to the elbow and pressed. Shoulder titles are worn on the epaulettes. The badges of rank are brass worn on a leather wristlet. The stable belt is narrow dark blue, yellow, wide red, yellow, narrow dark blue and the buckles are at the front. The regulations state khaki trousers only in this order of dress, but I have seen crimson worn. The head-gear for Officers and Warrant Officers is the officers' service dress hat or a crimson side hat. NCOs and troopers wear a side hat or the Royal Hussar brown beret with the regiment's badge on a crimson patch. Shirt sleeve order is worn during daylight hours only.

JERSEY ORDER. Officers and Warrant Officers wear the Royal Hussar pattern jersey which is dark green. The stable belt is not worn. Service dress hat and brown shoes. All others wear the khaki issue jersey with shirt and tie, khaki trousers and beret. The Officers' beret is also brown but the badge is the Prince of Wales' feathers without the inscription and is made of woven silver thread.

COVERALLS, COMBAT KIT, ETC. Normal issue. These are in fact about the only uniforms which are constant throughout the Army.

ABOVE: Button—flat with the design impressed. Arm badge and pattern of the Officers' beret badge. RIGHT: United Nations Force. Light khaki/sand tropical drill. The trousers are slightly greener than the shirt. Sky blue beret and cravat. UNO badges on beret and left arm. Stable belt and brass shoulder titles.

13th/18th Royal Hussars

(QUEEN MARY'S OWN)

NO. 1 DRESS: BLUE.

FACING COLOUR: WHITE.

AMALGAMATION:

APRIL 1922—18TH ROYAL HUSSARS (QMO) AND 13TH HUSSARS TO FORM 13TH/18TH HUSSARS.

REDESIGNATED:

DECEMBER 1935—13TH/18TH ROYAL HUSSARS (QMO).

FULL DRESS. See plate, page 48.

NO. 1 DRESS. *Officers.* Standard dark blue tunic and overalls. The officers' type is more fitted than that of the ranks'. It has a white collar and shoulder chains with the regiment's title 13/18RH in brass. There is no waist-belt, but a gold and silver cartouche belt worn over the left shoulder. The overalls have double buff stripes and the tunic is fastened with plain domed brass buttons. The forage cap is dark blue with a white top and the badge in brass.
Soldiers. Standard blue jacket worn without a belt, steel shoulder chainmail and white gorget patches. Blue trousers with double white stripes. Black boots or shoes. Blue forage cap with a white top or, when not on duty, a blue side hat with a white top. All badges (except QMO) and buttons are brass.

The band wear overalls, which are tighter than trousers, spurs and a white crossbelt with the regimental badge on the pouch. The same badge is worn on each of the white collar patches. Badges of rank are worn on the right sleeve only and are placed on white patches, except for WOs who have no backing to their rank badges.
QMO emblem: **1** WOs—half an inch below the badge of rank, embroidered in silver; **2** Sergeants—in silver, between the lower two of the three gold chevrons; **3** Corporals—in the centre of the chevrons.

SERVICE DRESS, OFFICERS. Khaki with three pointed buttoned breast pocket flaps, no pleat on the pocket. Horizontal hip pockets with rectangular

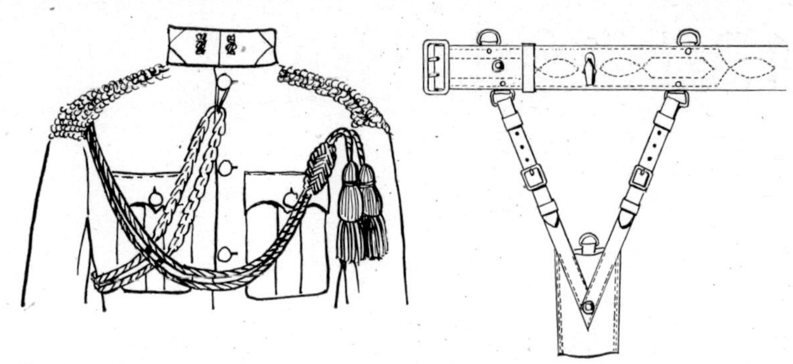

Bandsman's yellow wool cords and tassels.

Sword scabbard suspension straps fitted to the 'Sam Browne' belt.

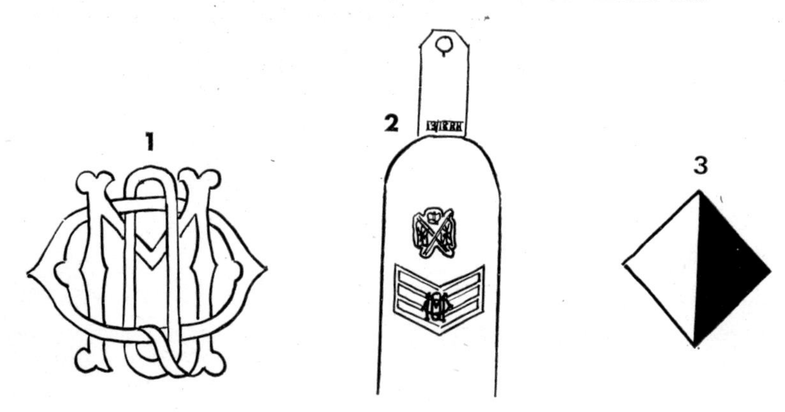

1. *Queen Mary's Own cypher in silver.* **2.** *Position of cypher for recruiting sergeants.* **3.** *White and dark blue flash, first worn on the sunhelmets on the 13th Hussars in the Boer War and subsequently worn in Mesopotamia and World War 2. It is now worn on left upper arm.*

buttoned flaps. All buttons are plain half dome in brass. Shoulder numerals and collar badges in brass. There are also two buttons on each cuff. Cavalry 'Sam Browne' with whistle. Trousers with turn-ups, brown shoes, forage or service dress cap.

NO. 2 DRESS, SOLDIERS. The usual issue type with the following embellishments: plain half dome brass buttons plus one on each cuff, brass collar badges and shoulder numerals, 13/18RH. The Regimental flash on the left upper arm with white portion to the front. A white lanyard around the right shoulder. The QMO cypher as described for No. 1 Dress. Warrant Officers' and Staff sergeants badges in brass. The cloth belt to the tunic is worn when working or walking out but it is optional in barracks. The Regimental pattern belt, (WOs brown, ORs white) which has a rectangular brass plate with the badge in the centre, is always worn with the forage cap. Other headgear is a beret or side hat. The Regimental Provost sergeant and staff wear special white plastic belts.

COMBAT DRESS. Normal issue. Puttees are used instead of web anklets. On training a blackened '37 pattern web belt or '44 pattern belt and pistol holster, the holster being worn on the left. The coveralls are black worn with a black web belt and brown puttees.

SHIRT SLEEVE ORDER as described elsewhere. The stable belt is narrow dark blue, white, broad dark blue, narrow white, dark blue, with the buckles to the centre. The officers' and WO's pullover is dark green vee-necked and standard issue khaki for others, who must also wear the stable or Regimental belt over it. Caps worn are either officers' SD, side hat or beret. The officers' side hat has gold braid around the blue part of the hat. The beret badge issued to officers is woven metal thread, gold QMO cypher, blue motto and red and gold crown.
Quarter guards. These are ceremonial or guards of honour. No. 2 Dress normally, but No. 1 or Full Dress on occasions. With No. 2 Dress a white blancoed web belt and pistol holster. White pistol lanyard and gloves, forage cap.
Attached personnel wear their normal uniform but with the 13/18 blue and white flash on their left arm.

Army Helicopter Pilots. Helicopters are used by the Royal Armoured Corps for aerial reconnaissance. The pilots are soldiers trained at the School of Army Aviation, Middle Wallop, and are either officers or are automatically promoted to temporary sergeants on acceptances. The pilot suit is drab green with rank stripes on the right arm, or officers' shoulder insignia. A normal flying helmet and, when not in the air, a pale sky blue beret with a black rectangular patch over the left eye. On the patch is worn the regimental badge of the particular pilot—eg Royal Scots Dragoon Guards (called 'the Wirly Jocks'), 13th/18th Royal Hussars.

14th/20th King's Hussars

NO. 1 DRESS: BLUE.
FACING COLOUR: YELLOW.
AMALGAMATION: APRIL 1922—14TH KING'S HUSSARS AND 20TH HUSSARS TO FORM 14TH/20TH HUSSARS.
REDESIGNATED: DECEMBER 1936—14TH/20TH KING'S HUSSARS.

FULL DRESS (SOLDIERS). See plate, page 48. Black pouch with brass eagle on oval brass plate badge.

NO. 1 DRESS (SOLDIERS). Dark blue, five brass buttons down front and two small buttons on breast pockets. Two lemon yellow stripes on overalls. Black shoes. Scarlet forage cap with black badge. Silver chains on shoulders, brass collar badges and silver crossed kukris, which signify the affiliation with the 6th Queen Elizabeth's Own Gurkha Rifles, below shoulder chains on each arm. Rank stripes, gold wire on red. Above the stripes, full rank NCOs wear the regimental badge on an oval silver background. Lance ranks, a black eagle on a brass oval. RSMs wear the badge under their rank patch. (See photo and colour plate), and also eagle collar badges.

OFFICERS' SERVICE DRESS. Khaki with brass regimental buttons. Note, in the photograph below, the cut of the pockets and the whistle on a leather strap attached to the Sam Browne belt. Jacket has a centre vent. Shoulder title, in brass, reads 'XIV/XXKH'. Khaki SD hat or scarlet forage cap with black Prussian Eagle badge with gold crown, sceptre and orb.

NO. 2 DRESS (SOLDIERS). Khaki. 4 regimental buttons down front and two smaller ones on breast pockets and shoulder flaps. Shoulder title, in brass, reads '14/20H'. Rank stripes on both arms with the regimental badge above the rank on right arm, silver crossed kukri and collar badges. White lanyard around left shoulder. Scarlet soldiers forage cap with an all black badge.

BARRACK DRESS OR PULLOVER ORDER. *OFFICERS, WARRANT OFFICERS AND STAFF SERGEANTS.* Forage cap, side hat or beret. The badge worn on berets by officers is the Prussian Eagle woven in gold wire. Dark green pullover, stable belt—blue, lemon, blue stripes—with buckles to the front. No. 2 or battle dress trousers, shoes, shirt and tie. Denim shoulder tabs, embroidered with rank pips for officers and sewn-on badges, on the left arm only, for WOs and Staff Sergeants.

SOLDIERS. Dark green or issue pullover. The rest is as above except for caps. The officers' side hat is trimmed with gold braid and the soldiers' is plain scarlet. The beret is standard dark blue, but the officers have a badge of woven gold wire and soldiers have a black eagle on a lemon yellow, oval patch.

SHIRT SLEEVE ORDER. *OFFICERS.* Forage cap, side hat or beret. Light khaki shirt with boxpleat pockets and slip on shoulder titles. Stable belt, No. 2 trousers.

SOLDIERS: BEST. Forage cap or side hat. Khaki flannel shirt worn open necked and with rolled sleeves. Stable belt, black shoes.

SOLDIERS: 2ND BEST. Beret or side hat. Khaki flannel shirt. Stable belt. No. 2 or battledress trousers. Boots. WOs and NCOs wear appropriate badges of rank on right arm.

TRAINING. Beret, combat trousers, khaki flannel shirt, boots DMS (Direct Moulded Sole), black webbing belt, gaiters, issue coveralls.

RSM S. Jude with the regimental colours. Note the badge under the rank patch and the caplines, which pass under the left arm and terminate at the back of the collar with a slip-knot as at the front. (Army Public Relations Office.)

Back view of No. 1 Dress. Note the 1908 pattern sword (see colour plates).

Saladins and ferets of the 14/20 Kings Hussars on amphibious exercise in Hong Kong 1971. (Army Public Relations Office).

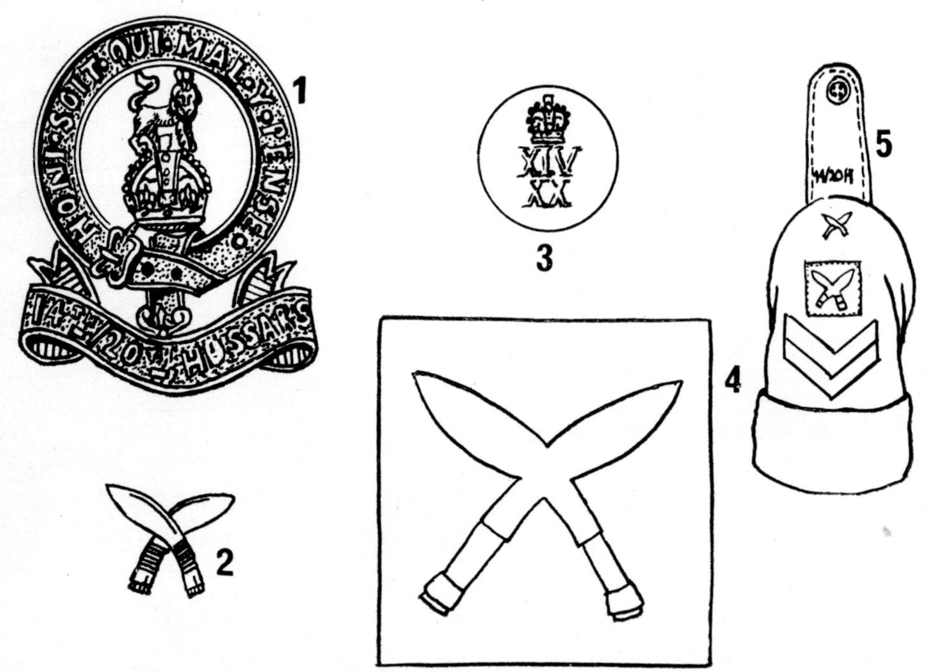

1. *Collar badge.* **2.** *Kukri badge.* **3.** *Regimental button.* **4** and **5.** *Formation sign of the 51st Gurkha Brigade worn on shirt sleeve order of Hong Kong based squadrons. (White on green).*

15th/19th The King's Royal Hussars

FACING COLOUR: SCARLET.
AMALGAMATION: APRIL 1922—15TH KING'S HUSSARS AND 19TH ROYAL HUSSARS (QUEEN ALEXANDRA'S OWN) TO FORM 15TH/19TH HUSSARS.
REDESIGNATED: OCTOBER 1932—15TH THE KING'S ROYAL HUSSARS.
DECEMBER 1933—15TH/19TH THE KING'S ROYAL HUSSARS.

FULL DRESS. See plate, page 48. Full dress is normally worn only by the band but it can be worn on special occasions such as guards of honour and weddings.

NO. 1 DRESS (BLUES). Blue tunic with shoulder chains which differ from the usual type insomuch as they are rectangular and on the shoulder only. Brass buttons, collar badges and no waist belt. A white cross belt with silver fittings and a black pouch bearing the regimental cypher is worn on ceremonial occasions. The blue overalls have two yellow stripes down each leg. Officers' 'Blues' have gold Austrian lace around the top and front edges of the collar.

OFFICERS' SERVICE DRESS. Khaki with four regimental buttons down the front and smaller buttons on the shoulder straps, breast pockets and lower pockets. There are two patterns of jackets. (a) box pleated breast pocket with three pointed flaps and horizontal square flapped lower pockets. (b) plain patch breast pockets with square flaps and the lower ones as above. Both types have a centre vent. The collar badges are of the Royal Crown surmounted by a lion, facing inwards, in brass. The officers' pattern is larger than that of the soldiers. Bright scarlet forage cap or khaki service dress hat.

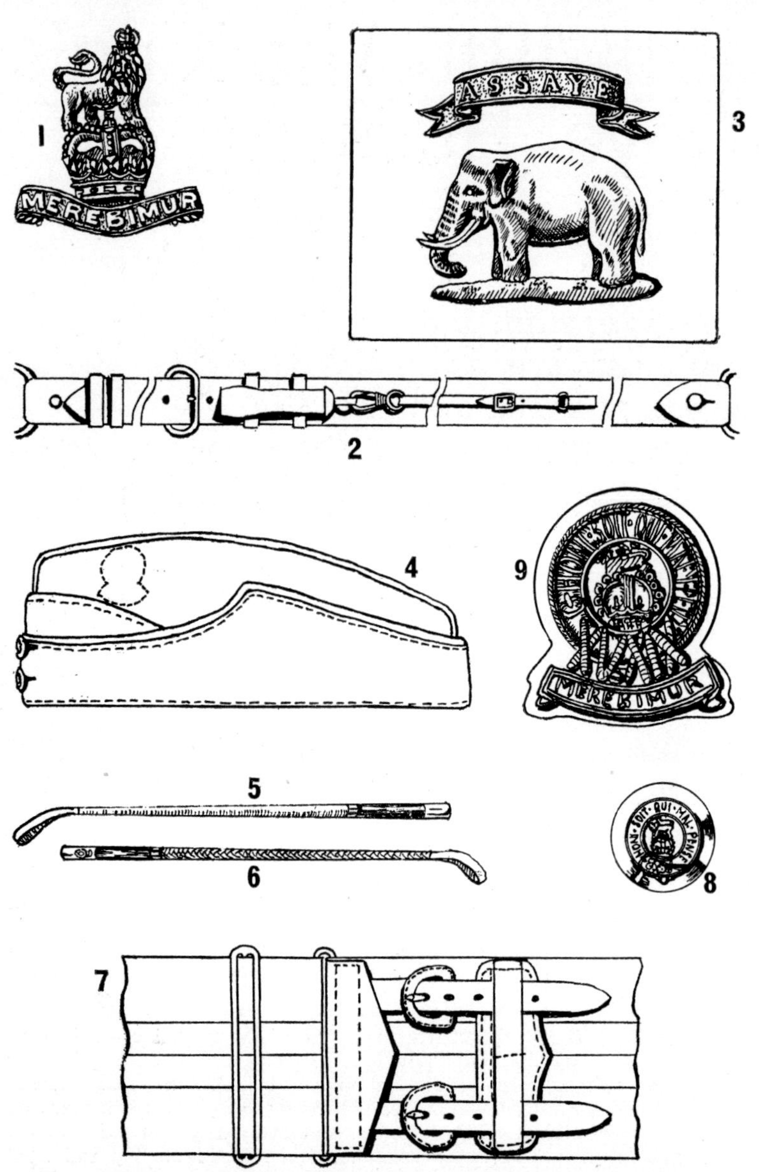

1. Collar Badge. 2. Officers' 'Sam Browne' cross belt. Silver whistle and attachment. All other metal is brass. 3. Troopers' and NCO's belt buckle. 4. Side hat of bright scarlet. Officers—gold piping, O/R's—yellow piping. Brass buttons with brass and silver badge. 5. WO II's whip, 2′ 9″ long. White end and bound shaft. Brown leather handle. Silver tip and ferrule. 6. Officers' whip. Plaited kangeroo hide. Silver tip and ferrule. 7. Stable belt—blue, yellow, red, blue. Light brown straps, etc. Chrome slides. 8. Regimental button, brass. 9. Officers' beret badge. A raised yellow silk garter, blue background to motto, all worked with gold thread. Silver crown and lion, crimson cap in crown with red and green jewels.

The officer in the middle is wearing the 1943 pattern tank suit. (Army Public Relations Office.)

'C' squadron of the 15th/19th King's Royal Hussars. The 'spirit of St. James' is named after Newcastle upon Tyne football ground. (Army Public Relations Office.)

A troop leader in the cupola of a Chieftain (Army Public Relations Office).

The cap badge has a gilt garter, a silver Crown and Lion and blue enamel motto with gilt lettering. The brass shoulder titles read 'XV.XIXH.' 'Sam Browne' belt with a silver whistle. Brown shoes with toe caps. A whip is carried.

NO. 2 DRESS SOLDIERS. Khaki, standard issue with brass regimental buttons. Collar badges have the brass crown and lion, as the officers', but smaller. The brass shoulder titles read '15/19H'. An arm badge of silver grey thread Crown and Lion is worn, on the right sleeve only, by: Sergeants and corporals—above stripes; S/Sergeants and SQMS—above stripes and below crown; WO II—below crown; WO I—below warrant badge. Bright scarlet forage cap with brass and silver badge. No lanyard. Black shoes. WO Is and WO IIs also carry whips. Orderly NCOs wear the white cross belt as described for No. 1 dress.

BARRACK DRESS OR PULLOVER ORDER. *Officers and WOs.* Forage cap, side hat or beret. Khaki round necked pullover, shirt and tie, stable belt (blue, yellow, red, blue), buckles to the front. Sewn on rank patches. Service dress or battle dress trousers. Officer's or WO's whip.

SQMS and below. Headwear as above. Standard issue jersey. No. 2 or battledress trousers. Stable belt. Black shoes.

SHIRT SLEEVE ORDER. As above except no pullover. Other ranks wear a brown plastic belt with a silver elephant and motto on a brass plate, which, incidently, is the only part of the uniform which has associations with the 19th Royal Hussars.

Overalls, battle dress, etc, are standard issue. A royal blue terry towelling cravat is worn with overalls.

Tank Commander: note the red patch behind the badge and the blue cravat (Army Public Relations Office).

A band of the 15th/19th King's Royal Hussars. Note the cross belt of the bandsman on the left, which is also worn by the Regimental Orderly Corporal, but with a black pouch and a silver regimental cypher.

Officer's Full Dress pouch, gold embroidery on scarlet. It is also worn with No. 1 Dress by the Orderly Officer after six in the evening. Other regiments have pouches of similar pattern—eg QRIH (see Chapter II for buckle detail).

16th/5th The Queen's Royal Lancers

NO. 1 DRESS: BLUE.
FACING COLOUR: BLUE.
AMALGAMATION:
APRIL 1922—16TH THE QUEEN'S LANCERS AND 5TH ROYAL IRISH LANCERS TO FORM 16TH/5TH LANCERS.
REDESIGNATED:
16TH JUNE 1954—16TH/5TH THE QUEEN'S ROYAL LANCERS.

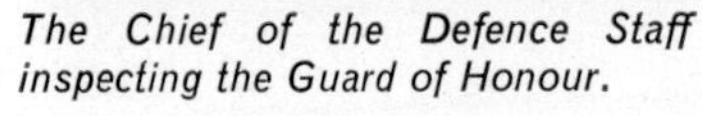
The Chief of the Defence Staff inspecting the Guard of Honour.

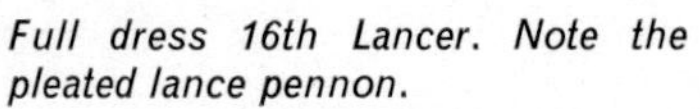
Full dress 16th Lancer. Note the pleated lance pennon.

FULL DRESS (16TH LANCERS). See plate, page 33.

5TH (ROYAL IRISH) LANCERS. Lance cap: black base with a scarlet top piped in yellow. The band dividing the two colours is yellow. The horsehair plume is green in a gilt holder. The boss below is yellow cord with a regimental button, on green, in the centre. Brass badge and chinchain. Yellow capline. Tunic: dark blue with red plastron, collar, cuffs and piping. Brass buttons and harp collar badges. Yellow and red girdle.

Overalls: dark blue with double yellow stripes. Black boots and swan necked spurs.

NO. 1 DRESS. The forage cap is scarlet with blue piping around the crown and at the quarters, the cap band is also blue. The badge is silver with the crown, lances and top half of the pennons in gold. WO IIs wear the smaller type officer's badge, which is the 16th Lancers collar badge. WO Is also wear this badge but with the officer's type forage cap. The jacket is dark blue with the usual shoulder chains, brass buttons, which are all the smaller pocket type, and regimental collar badges. Chevrons and other badges of rank, gold on blue, on the right arm only. The regimental arm badge is a silver harp and is worn by all NCOs or corporal and above. Sergeants and Staff Sergeants have it superimposed on the stripes with the crown above the top vee of the stripes. WOs wear it at the bottom of the right sleeve. All members of the band wear a gold lyre on the upper right arm and, in the case of NCOs, above the harp. The belt can be either the blue cloth belt that matches the jacket or the regimental yellow and red lancer's girdle. Blue trousers with double yellow stripes or, for the band, overalls.

OFFICERS' SERVICE DRESS. RAC pattern jacket (see RTR) with collar badges and shoulder titles in brass. Brown leather 'Sam Browne' and gloves. Light khaki soft collar shirt with a gold collar pin worn under the tie. Either the No. 1 dress hat, side hat or SD hat, depending on the occasion. Officers wear the cross strap of the 'Sam Browne' back to front, the reason being that when King Alfonso of Spain, Colonel of the Regiment from 1905 to 1941, arrived one day on parade with this cross strap reversed all the officers were ordered to wear their 'Sam Brownes' the same way, and have done so ever since. The shoes are brown brogue pattern.

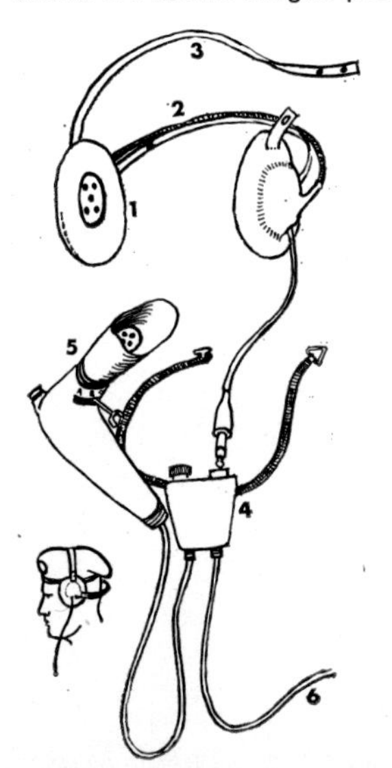

Tank crew headset. **1.** *Soft green rubber earmuffs.* **2.** *Wire spring and cable.* **3.** *Brown plastic head strap.* **4.** *Chest plate with canvas strap around neck.* **5.** *Black plastic microphone with green rubber mouthpiece.* **6.** *Lead to vehicle radio harness.*

1. *Collar badge in silver—the Harp and crown in the right circle is the pattern for the arm badge.* **2.** *Brass regimental button, 5th Lancers pattern.*

NO. 2 DRESS. No. 1 dress hat (forage cap) for parades and on other occasions, such as walking out or off duty, the Regimental side hat which is dark blue with a scarlet top and white crown piped in yellow. Only small brass buttons, of the 5th Lancer pattern on the tunic. The larger type normally used for fastening the tunic used only on the greatcoat. The cloth belt, issued with the uniform, has a brass buckle. 16th/5th Lancers collar badges on each lapel and '16/5L' titles on each shoulder strap. Rank chevrons are worn on both arms and the SQM's crown and the WO's badge are in silver embroidery and are of the regimental pattern. The regimental arm badge is worn as described in the paragraph on No. 1 dress, but in this case it is of silver embroidery. The regimental police wear, on their left arm, the provost arm band which is black with red 'RP'. All regimental orderly sergeants and regimental orderly corporals wear a white pouch belt when on duty. Warrant officers wear officer's service dress caps. WO IIs wear brown shoes. Crops are carried by squadron sergeant majors and provost sergeant.

SHIRT SLEEVE ORDER. Standard. The stable belt is, from the top, red/yellow/blue in equal stripes, with the buckles on the left hip. White tape rank chevrons sewn on to the shirt or brass badges on a leather wrist strap.

COMBAT KIT. The badge on the officers' beret is embroidered, as is the case in many regiments. The webbing belt is scrubbed and buff in colour, the kit itself is standard. Each squadron has its own cravat: **A** squadron—red; **B**—blue; **C**—yellow, **HQ**—green.

Pattern of the officers' tunic showing the back to front cross strap and the shirt and collar pin.

17th/21st Lancers

NO. 1 DRESS: BLUE.
FACING COLOUR: WHITE.
AMALGAMATION: APRIL 1922—17TH LANCERS (THE DUKE OF CAMBRIDGE'S OWN) AND 21ST LANCERS (THE EMPRESS OF INDIA'S) TO FORM 17TH/21ST LANCERS.

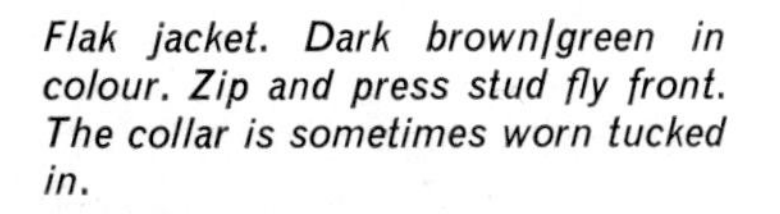

Flak jacket. Dark brown/green in colour. Zip and press stud fly front. The collar is sometimes worn tucked in.

Trumpet Major in No. 1 Dress and the sleeve badges of the Bandmaster. The banner is dark blue with silver badge and fringe. The upper halves of the lance pennons are red.

1. *Button.* **2.** *Stable belt. All silver buckle with the woven cloth belt in dark blue and white.* **3.** *Regimental Police arm band. Brass letters, silver badge worn on the right arm above the elbow.*

FULL DRESS. See plate, page 33. NCOs have gold chevrons on white patches, on the right arm only. Full rank NCOs wear the 'Death's Head' badge on top of the chevrons and WOs under their badge of rank on the forearm. Senior NCOs also wear gold braid around the top edge and front of the collar and around the top of the cuffs. For officers, substitute gold for yellow on all cords and piping. They also have two bands of gold around the base of the lance cap and on the peak, plus a white cock's feather plume instead of horse-hair. The cartouche belt, worn by all officers in Full or No. 1 Dress, is gold braid with a centre stripe of white. The buckles, chains and pickers and the cartouche itself are silver. This belt is worn from the left shoulder, over the caplines which come from the right shoulder. Finally, plaited gold shoulder straps, on which are worn the rank badges. This uniform, as for most regiments, is worn only on special or historical occasions.

NO. 1 DRESS (BLUE PATROLS). *Officers and Senior NCOs.* Blue jacket with brass buttons, two on the cuffs. Steel shoulder chainmail and silver 'Death's Head' collar badges. Blue overalls with double white stripes. Wellington boots and spurs. No. 1 Dress hat and white kid gloves. Officers, and on occasions the RSM and bandmaster, also wear the cartouche belt, sword slings from under the jacket, plated sword scabbard with 1912 pattern sword and gold braid sword knot.

Junior NCOs. Blue jacket with white gorget patches on the collar—by custom these are not worn by officers and WOIs. Collar badges, shoulder mail and brass buttons. Blue trousers with double white stripes and black shoes. No. 1 dress hat. Chevrons are gold on white patches. Full rank NCOs and WOs wear the arm badge immediately below their rank insignia. The dress hat is dark blue with a white cap band and white piping around the crown and the quarters of the crown.

OFFICERS' SERVICE DRESS, PARADE ORDER. The tunic has box-pleated breast pockets with single pointed flaps, the hip pockets have rectangular flaps and all are buttoned. There are also two small brass buttons

ABOVE: 17th/21st Lancers' vehicles showing HW, A, B and C squadrons plus support vehicles. The squadron signs are HQ: Diamond, A: Triangle, B: Square, C: Circle.

on each cuff. Gilt 'Death's Head' collar badges and bronze badges of rank on the shoulder straps. Parade order differs from normal service dress in that a sword, with a brown leather scabbard and sword knot, is suspended from the 'Sam Browne' belt. The shirt and tie are a very pale khaki and the gloves and shoes are brown. The No. 1 Dress hat only is worn with this order of dress.

NO. 2 DRESS, SOLDIERS. The standard tunic is worn without a belt. There are no shoulder titles or lanyard, the only distinctions being the 'Death's Head' collar badges in silver and the NCO's arm badge. On parade the SMG, without its magazine, is carried. This is the standard personal weapon of the RAC.

TRAINING ORDER. Combat kit, coveralls or tank suit, boots, beret, black web belt, pistols for commanders and SMGs for others.

The Royal Tank Regiments

1ST, 2ND, 3RD, 4TH

NO. 1 DRESS: BLUE.

FACING COLOUR: BLACK.

Being a comparatively new regiment, its history dating from 16th February 1916, the 'Tanks' do not have a Full Dress uniform as do other members of the RAC. In the Regiment's short life it has probably gained as many battle honours in World Wars 1 and 2 as other regiments have in 150 years.

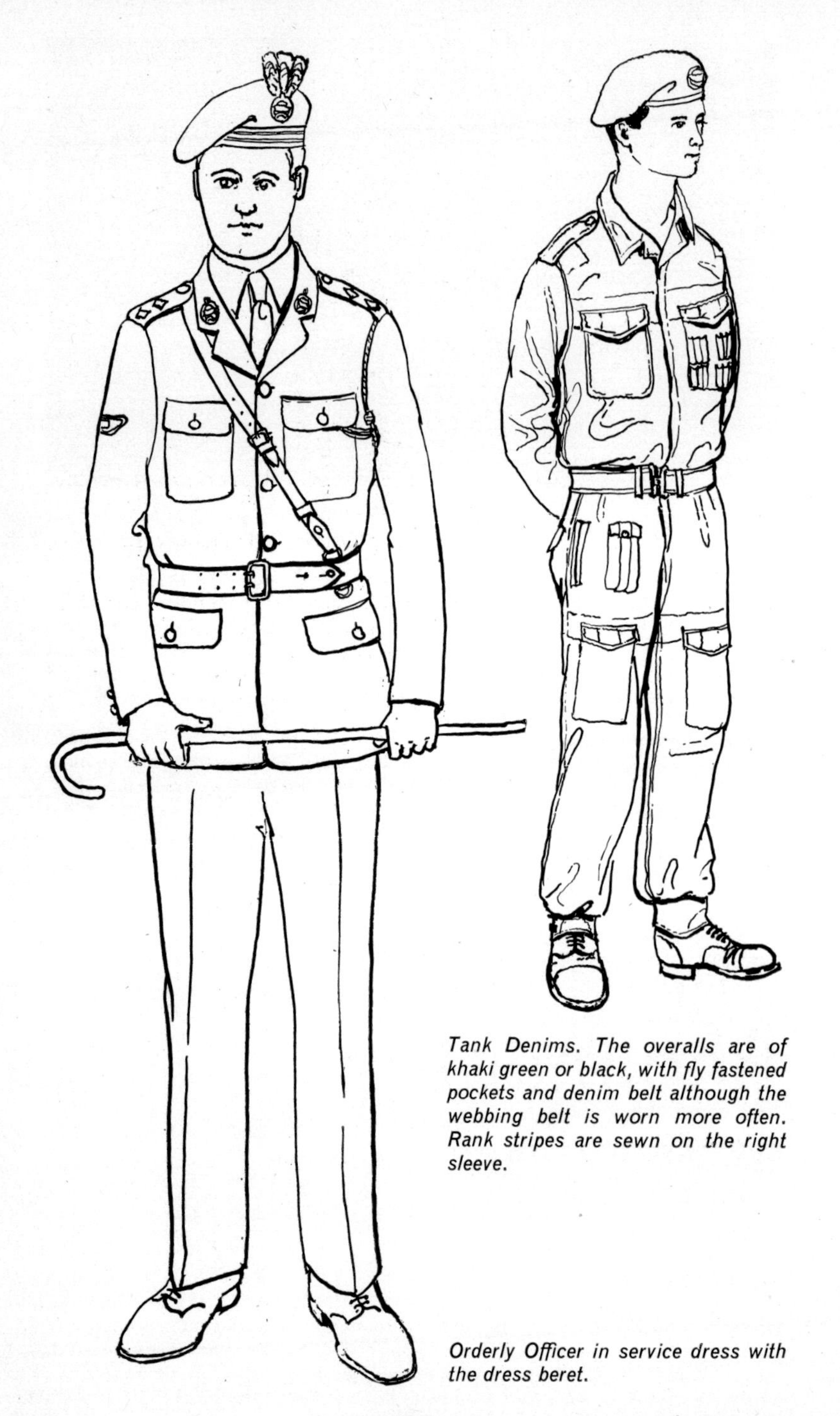

Tank Denims. The overalls are of khaki green or black, with fly fastened pockets and denim belt although the webbing belt is worn more often. Rank stripes are sewn on the right sleeve.

Orderly Officer in service dress with the dress beret.

1. *Bandsman: yellow wool aiguillette and light gold braid.* **2.** *No. 2 Dress.* **3.** *DPM Combat suit.*

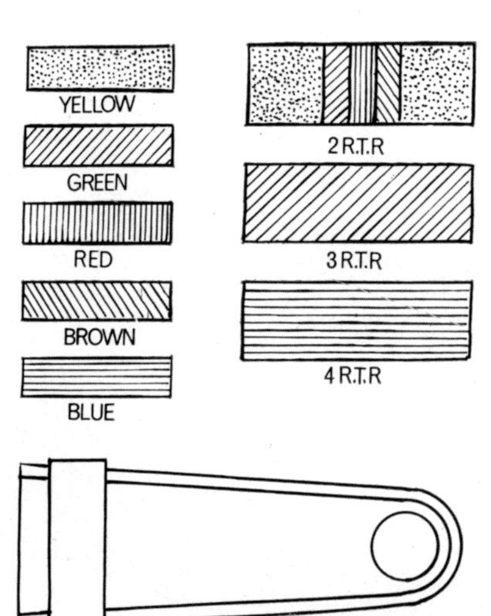

RTR shoulder strap flashes. The 1st Regiment do not wear a flash, instead they have a red lanyard.

NO. 1 DRESS. A Ministry of Defence directive dated 1971 discontinued the official wearing of No. 1 Dress except for General Officers. Although it is still unofficially used by certain ranks in other regiments, the RTR equip only the band in 'Blues'.

Officers. Dark blue tunic with five brass buttons down the front. Pleated breast pockets with three pointed flaps fastened with a button. Hip pockets are patch type with three pointed flaps and no buttons. There are two 4½ inch side vents to the jacket. The plain shoulder straps are detachable to allow gold plaited shoulder cords to be worn on ceremonial occasions. The silver embroidered 'Tank Crew' badge is worn 4 inches down from the right shoulder seam. On each side of the stand-up collar is a small version of the Regimental badge with the guns facing inwards. The RTR wear a black 'Sam Browne' belt and when a sword is carried it is the infantry pattern in a black scabbard with a black leather strap and acorn sword knot. On ceremonial occasions gold shoulder cords, a waist sash and a silver plated scabbard are worn. The sash is gold with two black lines running through it. On the left side it is tied in a small bow and the ends of the sash hang down, terminating in a black and gold fringe. The sword knot for this order of dress is gold and the scabbard is suspended from under the skirt of the tunic. The head-dress is a black beret of imitation astrakhan with a black cloth band, upon which is superimposed a band of black mohair braid, ¾ inch wide, edged top and bottom with gold piping. The badge is in silver embroidery from which issues a hackle in the regimental colours of brown, red and green. The brown feathers are on the left.

The first time that these colours were used was at the Battle of Cambrai, 20th November 1917. A flag was made of the only plain coloured silk to be found near the 'Tanks' HQ and was carried on the centre tank of the line 'Hilda'. General Elles was a passenger on this tank and his association with the Battle of Cambrai and the flag has become famous. The colours have given rise to the RTR motto: 'Through mud and blood to the green fields beyond'. The uniform is completed with dark blue trousers with a 2 inch black stripe, black gloves or white for ceremonial order.

Soldiers. The distinctions on the normal 'Blues' are silver collar and arm badges, gold chevrons on black and single black stripes on the trousers. Black RTR beret with silver badge and feather hackle. Shoulder chains are not worn.

Shoulder title and button, both in brass. The shoulder title is worn only on tropical shirt sleeve order.

SERVICE DRESS. Khaki, brass buttons, bronze collar badges, black 'Sam Browne', black beret (the Orderly Officer wears the dress beret), black gloves, shoes and socks. Officers of the Royal Tank Regiment carry an ash walking stick, which is also known as the (Ash Plant) or the (Stick). The tunic used to be the infantry pattern, but now the official standardised type is the RAC pattern based on the cavalry tunic. All officers wear the regiment's lanyard and those not on the strength of a particular Royal Tank Regiment wear a black lanyard, ie, Home Headquarters, senior officers, etc.

NO. 2 DRESS. Standard issue with brass buttons and silver collar badges. A white and black woven 'Tank Crew' badge is worn on the right arm. A wide black patent leather finish belt with a brass plate and the silver badge in the centre is worn with Best Dress. Black beret, badge and hackle. The four regiments are distinguished by their respective lanyards: 1st—red: 2nd—yellow; 3rd—green; 4th—dark blue. Sergeants and above carry a black cane with a silver knob. Only black socks, boots or shoes are worn.

PULLOVER ORDER. The pullover for officers, sergeants and above is black. The officers of 1st RTR have black shoulder boards with their rank insignia on them, those of the 2nd and 3rd RTR have black boards with their individual flashes and those of the 4th RTR have all dark blue boards.

SHIRT SLEEVE ORDER. Officers have a light khaki shirt, as do NCOs but of a slightly different pattern and material. Regimental lanyards are worn in this order of dress. The stable belt, which buckles on the left hip, is from top to bottom green, red, brown. You will notice that the RTR colours are always shown in the reverse of normal order, ie, right to left not left to right.

COVERALLS OR TANK DENIMS. These are always black in the Royal Tank Regiment. Other regiments have been known to wear black but it is now officially reserved for the RTR only. Coloured cravats are worn on exercise to distinguish the regiments: 1st—red; 2nd—yellow; 3rd—green; and 4th—dark blue. All webbing is black. It has been known for the Tank badge to be worn on the arm, unofficially. Rank chevrons are sometimes made up of white tape.

COMBAT DRESS. Standard issue denim or DPM suits (Dispersed Pattern Material, ie, camouflage). Regimental shoulder flashes are worn. There is an interesting story explaining why the 1st RTR wear a red lanyard instead of a shoulder flash. Up to 1941 they used to wear a red flash but in that year they were posted to Egypt. Unfortunately the South African Army wore a similar shoulder patch, which led to some confusion. It was then that they took to wearing the red lanyard, which continues today.

Junior Leaders Regiment and Parachute Squadron

ROYAL ARMOURED CORPS.

NO. 1 DRESS: BLUE.

FACING COLOUR: YELLOW.

The Junior Leaders Regiment, RAC, take in boys between 15 and 17 years of age with the aim of producing Warrant Officers and Senior Non-commissioned Officers. It is, in fact, an army technical college and the boys are taught trades similar to those taught in civilian colleges. At the age of 17½ they go to the regiment of their choice.

NO. 1 DRESS. About the only ones to wear this are the band. Junior bandsmen are trained here before joining their regiments. The forage cap is red with a yellow band, piped black top and bottom, and a silver RAC badge. Dark blue tunic, brass buttons, shoulder chains and silver collar badges. A white leather waist belt fastened with a brass, boy scout type buckle. Dark blue trousers with a single yellow stripe down the sides. Black boots or shoes. Lance Orderlies (parade ground markers) wear a black plastic pouch with a white plastic crossbelt. The pouch has a badge of crossed lances and a tank (made up of the 9th/12th Lancers and RTR badges).

NO. 2 DRESS. Around the left shoulder is a white plaited lanyard. The tunic buttons are brass and the collar badges are silver. The forage cap, or a dark blue beret with the RAC badge, are worn for the larger part of their stay with the Junior Leaders. In the last term the boys wear the uniform of their respective regiments. On ceremonial parades all Junior Leaders wear white woven plastic belts. Junior Orderly Sergeants also wear the crossbelt previously described. A coloured ribbon, denoting the squadron to which a Junior Leader belongs, is worn across the shoulder strap: A squadron—red; B—blue; C—yellow; D—green. Very small brass stars are worn on these ribbons to indicate a boy's progression: a junior—no star; intermediate—one star; a senior—two stars.

Officers and soldiers of the permanent staff wear the uniforms of their parent regiments, as they are only attached to the Junior Leaders Regiment.

PULLOVER ORDER. Boy soldiers wear a vee-neck fine knitted pullover with shoulder straps on which are worn the squadron ribbons. Off duty in barracks they have a crew neck sweater. It is red with two yellow bands around the top of the arms.

SHIRT SLEEVE ORDER. Squadron ribbons on the shirt shoulder straps. 'Dymo' type name badges are pinned over the left pocket. The stable belt has stripes of equal proportions, red, yellow, red.

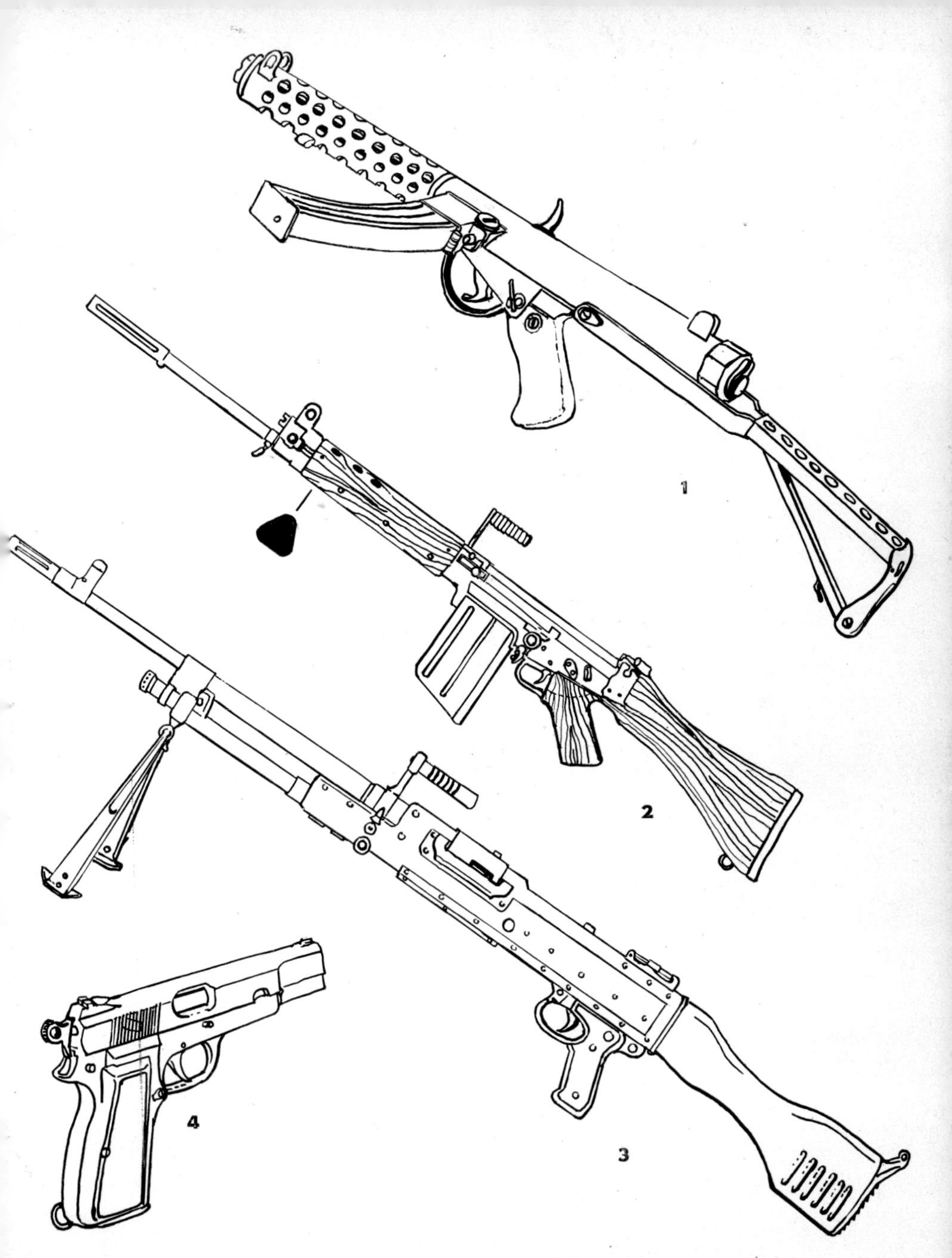

1. *9 mm sub-machine gun L2A3 (Sterling). Length: butt folded—19⅜ inches, butt extended—27 inches. 34 round magazine.* **2.** *7·62 mm rifle (FN) L1A1. 20 round magazine. Length 45 inches.* **3.** *7·62 mm general purpose machine gun (FN) L7A1. Length 49½ inches. 750 round per minute. Belt fed.* **4.** *9 mm pistol (FN) Browning. Length 7¾ inches. 13 round magazine.*

Pouch badge: brass lances and crown, silver tank. The bottom of the lance pennons are also silver.

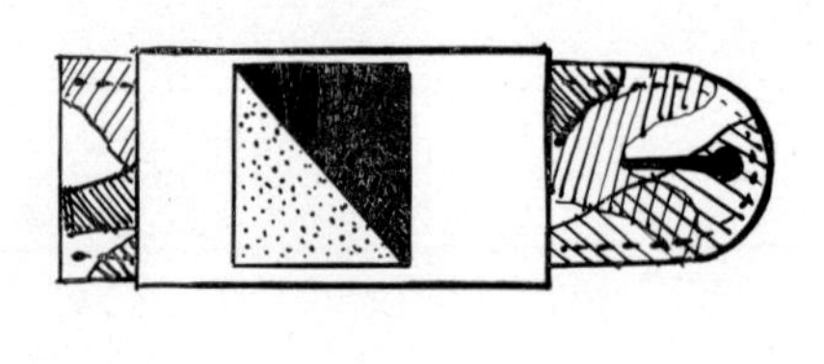

RAC training regiment instructors flash. Red and yellow square on a light khaki slip-on worn on both shoulders of working rig.

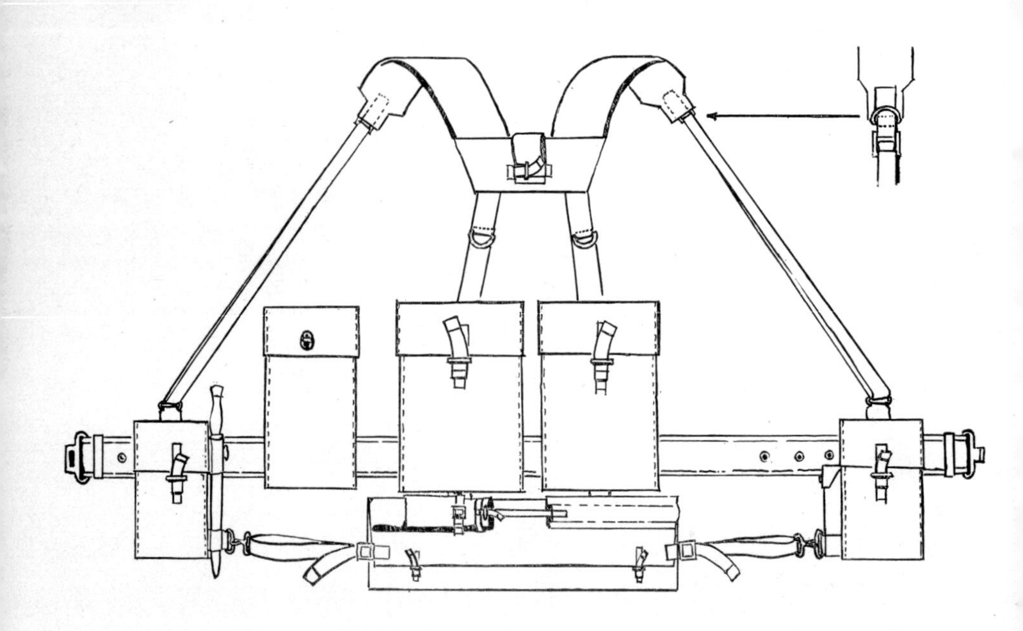

1958 pattern web equipment. Reading from left to right along the belt: ammunition pouch, bayonet, mess tin and water bottle, two small packs with groundsheet pack under, ammunition pouch. From the two 'D' rings a larger pack can be slung, and a pickaxe can be held in position by the strap on the Y piece of the harness and the two sleeves on the groundsheet pack, the haft going between the two small packs. All the webbing, including buckles, is finished in dark green.